# On Leadership, salad, and the American Revolution

James M. Triplett

On leadership, salad, and the American Revolution

ISBN: 978-0-578-01137-0

Published by: Dismal Realities

Erie, PA 16509 USA

www.dismalrealities.com

## Dedication

To my many students and friend, Lee Grable, who have challenged my views over the

years. I appreciate and have incorporated your feedback.

## Acknowledgements

As with any endeavour there are many who have contributed, knowingly or not, to the final product. At the top of the list are a close group of individuals who have influenced, challenged, and disagreed with my views, including my wife Michelle, brother Edwin, and friends Lee, Tom, and Ted. I have found relatively few instructors I agree with at this stage of my education and to those whom I do agree I thank you.

# Preface

The idea from this book came from my many learners who questioned the wide array of views on leadership. While I acknowledge the work of my predecessors in developing the subject of leadership – indeed, I could not have arrived at this point without them – it has been a view of mine that most are lacking singularly but that within many of them were the bases for a new theory. I do not buy into the view that leaders are great people; rather, good leadership is another way of saying they are aligned with the followers, structure, and environment. This may lead one to suggest many leadership successes are a result of simply being in the right place at the right time if this view is adopted and I cannot readily disagree. Some successful leaders may disagree but there is always room for exception as I have laid out in my Approximation Approach to research.

The salad bar idea came to me one day at one of those contemporary neighborhood bar and grille places one finds in a suburban mall area. Picking and choosing allows one to fit the end result to his or her satisfaction. In fact, one's satisfaction may be increased by choosing for him- or herself rather than accepting the one made for him or her, regardless of the variety. I suggest placing on the salad bar the good ingredients of leadership, as defined by their impact or staying power, and letting the user choose according to his or her unique attributes.

I leave this work for posterity to judge. Perhaps it will be a footnote to the field of leadership to which I would be grateful to be considered among those who came before me. Then again, perhaps there is something more to what I have derived. Let the journey begin.

# Table of Contents

Chapter I – The salad bar of leadership

The world of literature surrounding the notion of leadership may be characterized as a sea of potential explanations littered with the debris of academic and professional models – both empirical and conjecture – that may have been useful for a given point in time or situation. One is left wondering whether there is one defining view of leadership that may at least come close to being considered universal, if even 80% of the time is all one may realize. Indeed, the field of statistics allows one to accept hypotheses at the 0.10 or even 0.20 significance level based, in part, on the at times subjective view of the researcher. The prior statements led me to explore, both academically and empirically, whether there was a link between similarities and differences of leadership styles, defined through a liberal selection of established theories and complimented by the choices of which parts I found appealing much as one makes choices about what to eat at a salad bar in a contemporary restaurant. The result is a view on leadership that may, or may not, end up like the debris floating on the sea of possibilities previously mentioned; I leave that to the reader through the lens of empiricism to judge

What I had in mind during my frequent visits to the leadership salad bar was whether the congruency of the task environment, leadership style, and followership style of a given organization has any effect on its success at accomplishing identified goals and objectives. The purpose was to explore existing research on organizational task environments, leadership styles, and followership styles, expand on that research, and find ways to relate the general conclusions to successful leadership practices. The approach utilized was a case study of leaders, followers, and the environment of pre- and post-Revolutionary War America beginning in 1763 and continuing through 1794.

*Whetting the appetite.*

    The background for this research had its roots in the contingency approach to management but elements of relevant issues were found in research that addressed organizational design, the relationship between leaders, followers and the organizational structure, and the rights that leaders and followers possessed. The contingency approach research was conducted utilizing theories of Douglas McGregor (1987) and David R. Frew (1977, 1981, and 2002). Organizational design research was analyzed by studying the theories of Max Weber (1987), Frederick Winslow Taylor (1987), and Jay W. Lorsch (1987). The works of Mary Parker Follett (1987), Chris Argyris (1987), Rensis Likert (1987), Robert Tannenbaum and Warren H. Schmidt (1987), and David R. Frew (1977, 1981, and 2002) were reviewed to gain insight into the relationships between leaders, followers, and the organizational structure. The works of Thomas Hobbes (in Copleston, 1959) and John Locke (1988) were considered with respect to the reasons for the existence of government and the role of property and rights in the structure of a given organizational government.

    Max Weber's (1987) bureaucratic approach to organizational design and authority offered an efficient way to organize and manage the emerging forms of businesses that were growing increasingly larger and vertically oriented at the end of the nineteenth century. The division of tasks, development and implementation of rules and procedures, and a clearly defined hierarchical structure were the characteristics of this theory. The results were an organization that operated efficiently and provided equality to its members.

Mary Parker Follett (1987) suggested that there were essential aspects leaders should possess if they wanted to have a greater probability of achieving success. She added that leaders needed to train their followers to accept responsibility for their tasks and essentially be leaders as well. The combination of these was required for effective leadership.

Fredrick Winslow Taylor (1987) proposed a theory of management based on scientific principles that included a design of the organization to bring about democracy and co-operation between leaders and followers and proper selection of followers. This approach was beneficial for the leaders and followers as well as the organization. A redesign of the organization that allocated work among the leaders and followers established a feeling of co-operation between both parties. Proper selection of followers would ensure that the right employee was placed into the job best suited for them with high follower satisfaction and optimum productivity the result.

Douglas McGregor (1987) provided an analysis of leadership styles that fell on a continuum of autocratic and democratic styles. His basic premise was that followers had needs that were not being satisfied by conventional approaches. A realization that satisfaction of social and egoistical needs would help in the accomplishment of organizational goals and objectives would lead managers to restructure their approach to managing them.

Jay W. Lorsch (1987) suggested that there is no single ideal organizational structure because the design should be based on several dynamic factors that influence the organization from both inside and outside of it. The intent was to provide an overall dynamic approach to organizational design rather than a static cookie cutter one. An organization's structure could change from one type to another on the continuum of structures over a period of time based on the forces that influence it.

Chris Argyris (1987) focused on the interaction between individuals and the organizational structure, suggested that negative consequences were the result of different goals for each, and stated that a follower's given style was based on a continuum of human development. An organization's structure should be based on its objectives that are shaped by external forces while individuals approach a task with their own set of objectives. This was the essence of the conflict. The results of the inconsistencies between the two resulted in negative consequences such as frustration, lack of focus, and failure to accomplish organizational goals.

Rensis Likert (1987) offered his views on the rationale for linking individuals and their leaders in an organization, suggested that satisfaction drives performance, and felt that followers should be allowed to work to their ability. When this type of relationship existed between the two groups, followers became more productive because they felt a greater sense of self-worth and appreciation and thus wanted to work to their fullest potential. He felt that the greatest degree of supportive relationships could be found at the participative end of the continuum rather than the authoritarian end due to the higher degree of interaction and as a result the highest performance could be expected in this type of environment.

David Frew (1977, 1981, and 2002), a gifted professor of mine in the MBA program at Gannon University in Erie, PA, stated that leaders and followers have leadership and followership styles. The similarities between the styles and the task environment determined the degree of satisfaction that existed at any given time.

Personality was the primary influence of leadership and followership styles and was stable over short time periods while it was possible that it possessed some flexibility over time. The result was that an understanding of the task environment's structure should provide decision makers with the proper information to select leaders and followers who are ideally suited for employment in the given structure.

An alternate contingency leadership view was provided by Robert Tannenbaum and Warren H. Schmidt (1987) that focused on the forces that affect the interaction between leaders, followers, and the organizational structure. The interaction focused on the tradeoff between leader authority and the degree of control exercised in a given situation. A continuum similar in characteristics to the types offered by other contingency leadership theorists was utilized. Tannenbaum and Schmidt (1987) felt that leaders could and should move back and forth on the continuum and select behaviors or styles depending on how they perceived forces in themselves, their followers, and the environment. This stood in contrast to the theories adopted in this project thus far. Despite their views they offered insight into the short- and long-term interactions among the organizational forces, the trade-offs of authority and control, and personality influences on them.

Thomas Hobbes (in Copleston, 1959) felt that individuals who lived outside of any organized society did so in a manner where they had to survive on their own strengths and mental creativity and possessed the right to do whatever they chose. Those unable or unwilling to survive on their own agreed to give up a certain amount of rights to a society in exchange for security. The only notions of right and wrong were those defined by the societal contract while all other notions were reserved and defined by each individual person.

John Locke (1988) developed a theory of interaction between individuals' property and rights and the scope of laws that they were willing to give up in exchange for security. The degree of anxiety over loss of property and rights determined the amount of personal freedom of control over their life, property, and liberty that they ceded to a commonwealth.

*Deriving utility from the menu.*

The research on the interaction of the task environment and the leadership and followership styles provided for the existence of a continuum of the environment and each style that ranged from a simplistic, authoritarian, or autocratic end to a complex, participative, or democratic end. The congruence of the three with each other suggested that the result would be a higher degree of satisfaction among the participants than if the styles and structure were different. Although not the focus of this research, satisfaction, in turn, has been positively linked to an increase in productivity among other positive outcomes (Lawler and Porter, 1987, p.438). This applies to any organization whether its focus is public or private and its size is large or small. A satisfied American society was one where general prosperity, a lack of major social unrest, or general feelings of happiness and contentment, or any combination of them, existed. The extensions of this include the appropriate selection of leadership in countries the U.S. selects as part of its four Ds of foreign policy, specifically the democratization of nations. As I have found, it may not be appropriate to encourage democracy in some countries if the linkages between leadership, followership, environment, and structure are not in line. That is not to say that democratization should not be a long-term goal; rather, a realization that linkages affect satisfaction and that the personalities of leaders and followers as well as the time needed to change the structures suggest time, patience, capital and education are the prerequisites for change.

The concept of congruence is important because it is my belief that misalignment cr incongruency of the task environment may be a leading cause of organizational failure. Organizations – and nations - may at some point design or redesign their structure without considering the interaction between the objectives that shape the organizational structure and leader and follower styles. The organizational designer of today needs an integrated and prescriptive approach to both designing new organizations as well as redesigning existing ones in order to ensure future organizational success.

*Directions to the dinner plate.*

The approach taken was a case study of thirty-two years of American leadership, followership, and the task environment beginning in 1763 and continuing through to 1794. The period of time was examined in two-year increments to assess the degree of congruency both over a short term to see possible erratic swings in styles and a long term to determine the trend and direction of styles and the environment. There are some quantitative aspects to this approach but it was primarily qualitative in nature because it was felt that this method would be more suited to address the changes that took place over such a broad time frame. Gary Yukl (2002) favored this type of approach:

Most leadership studies only examine events that occur during a brief time interval, and there is a need for more longitudinal studies. Without such research, it is difficult to study leadership processes that evolve over time, or to assess the delayed effects of leaders on followers (p. 438).

It was important to choose a broad range of American history that focused on the leaders, followers, environment and resulting structure they interacted with in order to provide a better longitudinal study that could take into account very popular and mediocre leaders than would be possible with just one two-year period or decade. It also was positioned in order to look at the beginning of a perceived need for change in colonial America through the change process that included a few attempts at a new organization to a final form of government that has lasted for over 200 years.

Part of the success and longevity of the American government should be a result of a reasonable fit between the many leaders, followers, the environment and its structure. Yukl (2002) indicated as much by stating that "it is rarely possible to understand why an organization is effective by studying only a single, heroic leader" (p. 433). Analysis of leader and follower styles with the task environment should shed some light on whether congruency is important and what it means to the success of organizations. A detailed analysis of all three aspects through historical texts, literature, and statistical data from this period of time should confirm or refute the assertion put forth in this thesis. The ramifications should be applicable to many organizations in their attempt to successfully achieve their goals and objectives.

Chapter II – The ingredients

The items to include on the salad bar began with a look at the theories of ten individuals or group of individuals that provided background information and authority related to the organizational task environment, leadership styles, or followership styles, either separately or in combination with one or more of the other areas, and how they were related to the conceptual framework that the research proposal will follow. An analysis of David Frew's Leadership and Followership theory, along with his work on Perceived Task Complexity, forms the basis of the conceptual framework. The remaining aspects of the conceptual framework were developed by utilizing one or more aspects or research findings from the other theorists.

*Max Weber.*

The increased scale of operations, geographical spread of offices or divisions, affiliations with other companies, and the increasing diversity of products offered were some of the characteristics of the modern corporation which began to materialize around the end of the nineteenth century. Max Weber (1987) wrote on issues related to sociology, politics, and economics but he is most remembered for his literature that dealt with the ideal form of organizational structure in this environment. His work on organizational design and authority introduced the concept of administration of the organization and coordination of its tasks by rules and hierarchy, described the ideal structure, and indirectly provided some early hints of the existence of the task environment continuum.  Beneficial social consequences were a natural result of the

correct and successful implementation of a bureaucratic organizational structure.

The validity of legitimate authority was based on rational, traditional, and

charismatic grounds (Weber, 1987, p.7).  The fact that leaders occupied a position of

authority and exercised powers based on established rules and procedures was the

rational justification.  The validity of legitimate authority from the traditional point of

view derived from a follower's moral belief in obeying the designated leader who

exercised authority based an established framework of rules and tradition.  A leader's

claim to legitimate authority on charismatic grounds was based on "devotion to the

specific and exceptional sanctity, heroism or exemplary character of an individual person,

and of the normative patterns or order revealed or ordained by him" (Weber, 1987, p. 7).

A pure type of bureaucratic organization that utilized an administrative staff and

its overall effectiveness were based on a few "mutually inter-dependent ideas" (Weber,

1987, p. 8).  The first was that any rules or principles established for the organization

should be brought about based on either consensus or the need for expediency as well as

the degree of relevancy to the tasks that need to be addressed.  Rules and principles must

be abstract enough to allow general laws and procedures that are consistent with them to

be derived.  Weber (1987) added that "administration of law is held to consist in the

application of these rules to particular cases" (p. 9).  This led to the realization that a

leader who possessed authority as result of being in an office was bound by the laws that

existed for it.  The result was that the follower "who obeys authority does so, as it is

usually stated, only in his capacity as a 'member' of the corporate group and what he obeys is only 'the law'" (Weber, 1987, p. 9). The obedience was also only relevant to the follower with respect to the group that he or she belonged to and was not owed beyond it.

These ideas led Weber to offer a set of beliefs upon which his notion of legal authority rested. The first was the existence of an "administrative organ" whose functions were bound by the established, dynamic, and clearly defined rules in an organization where the functions were divided on the basis of their tasks (Weber, 1987, p. 9). This administrative organ was applicable to any organization regardless of its size, its orientation in terms of a single person, an appointed group of people, or an elected body of individuals, and whether or not it was a public or private entity. It was also applicable to any organizational structure on an autocratic-democratic continuum.

The structure of each office was such that each one was subject to the control of an office at a higher level. The presence of a grievance procedure which was available to organizational members from the lowest levels up to the top allowed everyone to have their concerns addressed in a fair and consistent manner.

The rules that officeholders operated under had to be in writing. Weber (1987) called this "formalism" and felt that this was necessary "otherwise the door would be open to arbitrariness" so therefore it was "the line of least resistance" (p. 16). The written rules also ensured that the office would not be shaped to fit a given person. Additional efforts to ensure that the officeholder was qualified and would exercise the proper degree of authority focused on keeping officeholders separate from owners, compensating them with an appropriate salary, providing a career path to the top, and communicating to all members that officeholders did not have a right to their office. Weber (1987) added that officeholders were "subject to strict and systematic discipline and control in the conduct of the office" (p. 12). Those in office were free to leave if they chose or they could be removed if their actions dictated it. They did not have the right to determine their successor as each was appointed by someone on a higher level.

The ones who occupied the offices also had to be technically competent with respect to the office that they held and they should be appointed not elected. The technical knowledge was any that provided expertise to the task at hand so that efficiency of operations was achieved. Weber (1987) felt that "the role of technical qualifications in bureaucratic organizations is continually increasing" and that "the only 'offices' for which no technical qualifications are required are those of ministers and presidents" (p. 12). The person who filled the top office in any organization was the only aspect of a bureaucratic organization that did not fit the pure type.

Those who sought to fill administrative offices had to demonstrate competence in the relevant functions carried out in it by either testing or certificates of competence. Once the competence was demonstrated they could be appointed. Weber (1987) preferred appointment to office because "election makes it impossible to attain a stringency of discipline" similar to appointees because when a subordinate runs for an office his chance of getting the office would not be based on the judgment of those higher in the organization (p. 12).

The fact that any type of organization could benefit from a bureaucratic structure did not prevent Weber from suggesting that there was one type that was the best. Weber (1987) felt that:

experience tends universally to show that the purely bureaucratic type of administrative organization – that is, the monocratic variety of bureaucracy – is, from a purely technical point of view, capable of attaining the highest degree of

efficiency and is in this sense formally the most rational known means of carrying

out imperative control over human beings (p. 14).

The monocratic form was one led by one individual who possessed knowledge relevant

to the tasks at hand and had a solid communications network in order to communicate

effectively down the hierarchical structure. This person exercised control based on this

knowledge but also from the knowledge gained while running it. The second form of

knowledge accelerated as the organization became more successful. This attainment was

the ultimate realization of a pure bureaucratic organization.

The implementation of a bureaucratic structure led to some favorable social

consequences. The first was a "leveling" of the requirements for those with technical

competence who sought employment at the organization (Weber, 1987, p. 16). It

eliminated the prevalent practice at the time of employment based on who a person knew.

The second beneficial consequence was an equality of treatment. This was

realized because "the dominant norms are concepts of straightforward duty without

regard to personal considerations" (Weber, 1987, p. 16). No longer would individuals be

singled out for unfair treatment solely on the basis of the personal preferences of

superiors.

The third result was based on utilitarianism on the part of the persons in higher

offices. Weber (1987) asserted that "it is the tendency of officials to treat their official

function from what is substantively a utilitarian point of view in the interest of the

welfare of those under their authority" (p. 16). This utilitarianism manifested itself in the

administration of the selected formal rules and laws. Weber (1987) felt that at this point an understanding of democracy would shed more light on the organization because the apex of bureaucratic administration would resemble democracy (p. 16).

Weber's bureaucratic structure was one based on division of tasks into a hierarchical structure that included a communications network to facilitate information flow up and down the structure. Formal rules and procedures ensure adherence by all members and brought about efficiency in operations and equality between members. He indirectly acknowledged the fact that there was no one best way to structure an organization although he favored a monocratic type. This type of organizational design was ideal when Weber developed it and with careful analysis it can still offer some insight into modern organizations and their structures.

*Mary Parker Follett.*

Mary Parker Follett (1987) developed a theory of leadership that offered suggestions for successful leadership. Four preconditions or requisites were outlined that if followed would lead to success. Followers should be adequately trained and given responsibility for their tasks as a way to accomplish the organizational goals and objectives.

A leader possessed four qualities or requisites that were necessary in order for success to be realized. The first requisite was "a thorough knowledge of [one's] job" (Follett, 1987, p. 52). This allowed leaders the ability to influence others because followers would be able to ascertain that the leaders were acting from a command of facets relevant to the task at hand. Since knowledge was possessed by leaders and followers alike it was possible for followers to exercise occasional unofficial leadership over one or more fellow organizational members. Follett (1987) added that "if such occasional leadership is exercised with moderation without claiming too much for oneself, without encroaching on anyone's official position, it may mean that person will be advanced to an official position of leadership" (p. 53). Leaders who progressed via this route possessed both knowledge of the task and prior leadership experience.

The second requisite was "the ability to grasp a total situation" which encompassed "facts, present and potential, aims and purposes and men" (Follett, 1987, p. 53). Leaders needed to be able to look at the whole picture and the relationships among various factors in the organization. The ability to do so increased with the span of control that a leader had. This leader was one who organized and directed the activities to accomplish the organizational goals and objectives.

The third requisite of leadership was the ability to understand the organization's current situation and reasonably foresee future events. Follett (1937) said that a leader's "wisdom, his judgment, is used not on a situation that is stationary, but on one that is changing all the time" (p. 54). A leader needed to be able to analyze data and draw conclusions that could be applied to the organization.

The final requisite was that a leader needed to be a risk taker. The leader did not need to take risks that bordered on extreme speculation as some gamblers might be prone to do. Follett (1987) suggested that leader's "spirit of adventure" could be described as "the insight to see possible new paths, the courage to try them, the judgment to measure results – these are the qualifications of the leader" (p. 55). This aspect of leadership was enhanced based on the amount and types of leadership experiences a given leader accumulated over time.

Follett (1987) then added another aspect of leadership that, although not a requisite, enhanced the effectiveness of a given leader's approach. This leader trained the followers to take responsibility for the aspects of the task environment in order to better accomplish their objectives. It involved delegating all necessary authority to them and provided opportunities for the followers to solve problems on their own. Follett (1987) added that "there are still men who try to surround themselves with docile servants – you all know that type – the ablest men today have a larger aim, they wish to be leaders of leaders" (p. 57).

Followers played a role in leadership as well by helping a leader lead the organization. The follower provided information and suggestions to the leader, corrected flawed leader directives when needed, acted responsibly, and adhered to organizational rules and regulations that were consistent with the goals and objectives. Follett (1987) stated "leaders and followers are both following the invisible leader – the common purpose" (p. 56).

Follett's (1987) leader was one who had experience and knowledge of a situation and could harness them to understand the environment and plan for future activities. This person was not afraid to take reasonable risks in pursuit of the planned goals and objectives. The successful accomplishment of them was increased when the leader involved the followers by providing training and responsibility.

*Frederick Winslow Taylor.*

Frederick Winslow Taylor (1987) is most famous for his insight into Scientific Management. The benefits of employing this technique were enjoyed by many types of people in diverse organizations. This revolutionary approach to management at the time of its implementation involved collecting and analyzing information about all aspects of an organization, selection of workers and their development, combining the science and the workers by offering incentives, and a redivision of all tasks between management and workers that focused on cooperative and democratic practices.

An initial feature of a change to Scientific Management by many organizations was an initial backlash by workers who feared that labor saving devices would cost them their jobs. Taylor (1987) stated that "even though that labor-saving device may turn out ten, twenty, thirty times that output that was originally turned out by men in that trade, the result has universally been to make work for more men in that trade, not work for less" (p. 34). Sometimes the result was violence and destruction brought against organizations that tried to improve output in a given industry. The implication was that people tended to cling to their established ways and were slow to change (Taylor, 1987, p. 38).

Leaders who followed the principles laid out by Taylor were able to avoid the violence and destruction that some organizations experienced. The workers and managers most likely realized the benefits of applying Scientific Management. Taylor (1987) added:

> the great good comes from the fact that, under scientific management, [the workers] look upon their employers as the best friends they have in the world; the suspicious watchfulness which characterizes the old type of management, the semi-antagonism, or the complete antagonism between workmen and employers

is entirely superseded, and in its place comes genuine friendship between both sides (pp. 37-38).

Confusion as to what Scientific Management was and was not forced Taylor to lay out his view of this approach to leader-follower relations and the drive for efficiency. It was not merely time and motion studies, a bonus system, or piece-work, but instead a change in the way that workers and their employers view each other (Taylor, 1987, p. 38). Scientific Management was a system that utilized the above tools to facilitate the change in the mental outlook of both parties. The change in outlook was so important to the success of this approach that Taylor (1987) cautioned:

> scientific management does not exist and cannot exist until there has been a complete mental revolution on the part of the workmen working under it, as to their duties toward themselves and toward their employers, and a complete mental revolution in the outlook of the employers, toward their duties, toward their duties, and toward their workmen (p. 38).

The four principles that Taylor established in order to implement Scientific Management were the collection of job-related knowledge, proper selection of workmen, combining workers and the science, and a redivision and reassignment of work between both groups. Successful results depended on the sequential implementation of these principles.

The first principle of Scientific Management was the voluntary gathering of all knowledge "which, in the past, has been in the heads of the workmen" (Taylor, 1987, p. 40). The effort had to be voluntary on the part of management because they were the ones who initiated the change. Initial problems of data collection could be overcome by persistent managers who put the workers at ease and gathered only information that was

critical to the task at hand. The relevant information was then reduced to work rules and

procedures that affected employees and managers were then expected to follow to the

letter.

The second principle of Taylor's was the selection of workers. Rather than hire

the cheapest labor available managers derived the best results by selecting qualified

workers and training them to be specialists. Taylor (1987) stated that "it becomes the

duty under scientific management, of not one, but of a group of men on the management

side, to deliberately study the workmen who are under them" in a meticulous manner and

then train and develop the workers to perform their tasks more efficiently (pp. 40-41).

Management was expected to follow up with higher wages to the employees as they

progressed.

Taylor's third principle was to combine the science with the workers through

incentives or an incentive system. This was a two-fold approach that involved offering a

reward or something worthwhile to the worker to make them come together with the

science and a second part which allowed the workers to leave if they did not want to

come together with it. Taylor (1987) added "select and train your workmen all you may,

but unless there is some one who will make the men and the science come together, they

will stay apart" (p. 41).

The redivision of the tasks in the organization's task environment into two parts

was the fourth principle. This division involved taking "all of that work which formerly

was done by the workmen alone" and dividing it into two sections with one going to

management and the other to the workmen (Taylor, 1987, p. 42). The result was cooperation between both parties to accomplish the work. Managers were responsible for their input into the work process and labor was responsible for theirs. Both sides knew who was responsible for what tasks and held each other accountable. Taylor (1987) added that "it is this real co-operation, this genuine division of the work between the two sides, more than any other element which accounts for the fact that there will never be strikes under scientific management" (p. 42). The ability of workers to hold managers accountable for their actions or lack of effort was at the time a novel approach.

Taylor's Scientific Management approach to workplace efficiency and beneficial relationships was successfully applied to many diverse organizations. His contributions to the field of organizational behavior and leadership were a careful analysis of the task environment, proper selection and training of employees to fit the environment, a realization of the need to get workers and managers to work toward shared goals and outcomes, and the benefits of resulting satisfaction of all members.

*Douglas M. McGregor.*

Douglas M. McGregor (1987) felt that the nature of the organization was among a few factors that affected human behavior. He defined the ends of the styles and task continuums as autocratic and directive Theory X at one end and democratic and participative Theory Y at the other. Conventional beliefs in management such as workers were lazy, had no ambition, did not like responsibility, and resisted change were reflected in "organizational structures, and managerial policies, practices, and programs" (McGregor, 1987, p. 129). These beliefs were built up over time prior to McGregor's research and were behind the design of traditional organizational structure and leadership practices. Theory Y was the belief that followers were capable of self-motivation if only the leaders provided the appropriate tools, leadership, and environment.

Theory X was one end of the continuum and was based on three primary and a few secondary beliefs. The first belief was that collection and management of resources toward organizational goals was the role of management. It was felt that followers were not capable or concerned with this end. McGregor (1987) felt that the second belief of management relative to the followers was that their function was "a process of directing their efforts, motivating them, controlling their actions, modifying their behavior to fit the needs of the organization" (pp. 128-129). The second belief led to the third belief that without direction followers would not accomplish organizational goals and objectives. McGregor (1987) added that "people would be passive – even resistant – to organizational needs" and as a result "they must therefore be persuaded, rewarded, punished, controlled – their activities must be directed" (p. 129).

The secondary beliefs were not as prevalent nor were they inclusive. Followers were considered to be lazy, avoided responsibility, were "resistant to change", "not very bright, the ready dupe of the charlatan and the demagogue", and did not like change (McGregor, 1987, p. 129). The most effective managers and the ideal organizational structures were the ones that were able to direct and control the followers.

There were a range of possible approaches that managers employed within the Theory X model. The hard approach involved "coercion and threat (usually disguised), close supervision, [and] tight controls over behavior" while the soft approach involved "being permissive, satisfying people's demands, [and] achieving harmony" (McGregor, 1987, p. 129). While the soft approach sounded more desirable it was still directive in nature. The end result sought was still to get followers to acknowledge direction and submit to it. Problems resulted though as the hard approach led to follower resentment and possible reduction of output and services while the soft approach led to followers taking advantage of the reduction in management activities.

The reason for the inadequacy of Theory X was found in the study of what motivates human beings and a needs hierarchy that humans progressed upward as needs were satisfied (McGregor, 1987, p. 130). The lowest need was physiological followed by safety, social, ego, and self-fulfillment. When a need was satisfied, the next one became the focus of an individual and as such the needs that were satisfied were not capable of motivation.

Physiological and safety needs were generally satisfied by employment and wages, working conditions, and benefits so that left the average followers seeking to satisfy the remaining needs. The failure to provide means for followers to satisfy these needs was the reason behind management's beliefs in Theory X principles. It became the role of management to satisfy the unmet needs. McGregor (1987) said that "direction and control are essentially useless in motivating people whose important needs are social and egoistic" so management needed to use a different approach (p. 133). The result was Theory Y.

Theory Y was the other end of the continuum and is characterized by four principles. Management, as in Theory X, had responsibility for organization of the productive resources, followers were not passive, motivation was present in everyone, and "the essential task of management [was] to arrange organization conditions and methods of operation so that people [could] achieve their own goals *best* by directing *their own* efforts toward organizational objectives" (McGregor, 1987, p.133). The

realization of these principles called for management to alter the way they got their

followers to accomplish tasks. Rather than directing them, managers provided the

necessary tools and created an environment that was conducive to allowing followers to

satisfy their needs. The change to Theory Y, with its focus on follower "self-control and

self-direction," from Theory X, with its "exclusive reliance upon external control of

behavior," involved time as the followers "have been conditioned by [their] experience

under [Theory X]" (McGregor, 1987, p. 134).

McGregor acknowledged both ends of the authoritative-participative continuum

but he clearly favored the Theory Y approach as the ideal one in which leaders and

followers interacted within the organizational structure. The emphasis on satisfying

follower's needs allowed managers to successfully accomplish the goals and objectives

of the organization. The one caution in the application of Theory Y would be that people

differ with respect to their needs and this variability may make it difficult to satisfy

everyone's needs. Management must then select a general approach to satisfying needs

that will affect the largest percentage of followers. The most important thing for

managers to keep in mind though is the overall intent to satisfy follower needs to the best

of their ability.


*Jay W. Lorsch.*

Jay W. Lorsch (1987) suggested that there was no single ideal organizational

structure because the design should be based on dynamic external factors, the tasks at

hand, coordination of subunits, and the characteristics of the people involved. He offered a way of thinking about organizational structure instead of a one best approach. External forces such as technology and market demands were major factors that ranged from simple to complex and static to dynamic and as a result no single structure was well suited to all organizations.

Lorsch made a distinction between the basic structure of an organization and its operating mechanisms. Lorsch (1987) stated:

> design of the *basic structure* involves such central issues as how the work of the organization will be divided and assigned among positions, groups, departments, divisions, etc., and how the coordination necessary to accomplish total organizational objectives will be achieved (p. 201).

Aspects of the structure were communicated to the members of the organization through items such as organizational charts, job descriptions, and orientation programs for new hires. These organizational tools should not be relied on solely to communicate to the employees but should be supplemented by other relevant ones.

Operating mechanisms were utilized by managers to further communicate and provide a feedback channel from the employees that helped improve the chances the goals and objectives behind the structural design were accomplished. Lorsch (1987) added that "operating mechanisms include such factors as control procedures, information systems, reward and appraisal systems, standardized rules and procedures, and even spatial agreements" (p. 201). Caution needed to be exercised to ensure that operating mechanisms were consistent with the basic structure as the results were less than optimal if they were not.

Lorsch (1987) said that differentiation, the functional and managerial difference of departments in an organization, and integration, the degree of collaboration among the departments, were key concepts of the structural design (p. 204). Examples consisted of the internal and external forces that affected marketing considerations, engineering concerns, and production issues that surrounded each product or service an organization offers to a customer. Differentiation among the departments was based on the amount of certainty of available information that each department possessed relative to a given product or service. Lorsch (1987) added that "how similar or different these parts of any environment were on the certainty-uncertainty continuum determined whether that environment was relatively homogeneous or diverse" (p. 205). Thus forces in the environment external to the organization determine the degree of differentiation and integration of a firm. Once these are known the design of the structure can begin.

A sequence of steps was developed to allow designated parties to design a proper organizational structure. Lorsch (1987) added that designers "should be aware that in practice it is necessary to move back and forth among them as one thinks about the whole problem of structural design in a given organization" (p. 212). How an organization moves through the steps and in what order depends on the external forces that affect it.

The first step was to group organizational tasks into units or departments based on the differentiation and integration concepts. Units with similar tasks and functions should be grouped together because one unit's aspects and tasks may reinforce another unit's tasks while simplifying the coordination activities of the leader (Lorsch, 1987, p. 212). Units that may be required to integrate activities should be grouped together as well in order to facilitate accomplishment of the common goals across the entire organization.  Each unit may have some degree of differentiation and integration that force a designer to make a judgment call as to whether it is grouped more on the basis of differentiation than integration or the other way around.

The second step in the design of the organizational structure required the design of integrative devices.  Lorsch (1987) said "a primary integrative device in any organization is the management hierarchy" and that in the progress of designing one "we are essentially making choices about which units we want to integrate through the hierarchy" (p. 212).  Other devices that facilitated integration among units were cross functional teams and specialists who were able to provide input to all units involved in a joint effort.

The third step of the design process involved the structure of the units.  This was the area of the process where operating mechanisms were introduced.  Motivation was a main consideration in this stage so design of reward and feedback mechanisms that promoted it in a manner consistent with collaboration at both the unit and organization-wide level were addressed and added.  Rules and standardized procedures relevant to the tasks at hand were also designed and implemented.  Lorsch (1987) added that "the unit hierarchy and spans of control should be designed not only to provide the intra-unit coordination required by the task, but also to encourage involvement in decision making at the level where the relevant information is available" (p. 213).

The characteristics of people were a final consideration with respect to conflict resolution.  Individuals who were assigned the task of working as an integrator between units were required to be able to effectively resolve conflict.  Another issue was whether operating mechanisms "induce unnecessary conflict" or if it was possible that "they cause organization members to see conflicts as win-lose rather than integrative" (p. 213). The designer should attempt to change the operating mechanisms in such a way that will persuade organizational members to resolve conflict. If all else failed, training in conflict resolution sometimes led to ideal results.

Lorsch suggested that organizational structure was the result of a careful analysis that involved external forces, the tasks necessary to accomplish the goals and objectives, the coordination of subunits, and conflict resolution skills of members. He offered a framework of structural design rather than a single approach to designing organizations. Careful attention to all stages of the design process should allow one to develop a structure that is well suited to accomplish its stated goals and objectives.

*Chris Argyris.*

Chris Argyris (1987) was concerned with the inconsistencies between research and models that focused on the interaction between followers' personalities and the organization's structural design. He set out to analyze the relationships and develop a useful model organizational designers could use to structure an organization's task environment and accommodate followers' personalities.

The focus of the research was based on the personality of followers and the organizational structure. Argyris began with a summary of personality. He stated:

personality is conceptualized as (1) being an organization of parts where the parts maintain the whole and the whole maintains the parts; (2) seeking internal balance … and external balance; (3) being propelled by psychological … energy; (4)

located in the need systems; and (5) expressed through abilities (Argyris, 1987, p. 141).

This definition of personality was followed by operational definitions that were derived from observations. Argyris (1987) felt "the self … tends to develop along specific trends" that started with a passive and dependent infant state and progressed toward an active and independent adult state, developed from a capability of a few behaviors to many dynamic ones, and from an erratic "short-time perspective" as a child to a deep "longer time perspective" (p. 142). The above characteristics allowed Argyris to plot an individual's profile, which he called an individual's self-actualization, along a continuum. An individual will progress from the dependent end on the left toward the independent end on the right, but with varying rates of progress and an ultimate end point somewhere in between the two extreme end points.

Argyris then turned to an analysis of organizations and their structures. Organizational design was traditionally addressed through rational processes. Argyris (1987) stated that "organizations are formed with particular objectives in mind, and their structures mirror these objectives" (p. 144). The problem was that followers with their diverse personalities may not fit the desired goals and objectives and thus the organizational structure. Argyris supported the prior research by earlier people such as Fayol and Taylor and determined that since no one to this point had offered a better alternative to proper organizational design then these types of theories should be more readily accepted. Organizations then needed to be planned and designed with follower personality in mind. Existing organizations required "modifying the ideal structure to take into account the individual and any (environmental) conditions" (Argyris, 1987, p. 145).

Task specialization in an organization focused on finding the most efficient way to perform a task or a given set of tasks. The refinement of tasks to those that required relatively few human skills "violates two basic givens of the healthy adult human personality" because it "inhibits self-actualization and provides expression to a few, shallow superficial abilities that do not provide the 'endless challenge' desired by the healthy personality" (Argyris, 1987, p. 147). A careful consideration of the follower's response to the design of tasks was critical if the desired result was satisfied followers and efficiency of output.

Once the tasks were designed the hierarchical structure was addressed so that control was exercised over all the tasks in order to ensure that they fit together to produce a final product or service. The designers needed to address motivation by assigning authority and tools to the leaders that allowed them to accomplish both motivational and organizational goals. Argyris (1987) suggested that this was a problem because "the individuals have little control over their working environment" while "at the same time their time perspective is shortened because they do not control the information necessary to predict their futures," which ultimately inhibited growth needs of personality and "exemplify in adults the dimension of immaturity" (p.148). Specialized tasks did not provide for growth so many organizations chose to compensate in other ways for follower dissatisfaction. Thus both motivation and organizational goals were not achieved.

Span of control became an issue in the course of organizational design. The number of employees under a supervisor was important because the more that are managed the less likely that close supervision results. Argyris (1987) stated that a "span of control ... will tend to increase the subordinate's feelings of dependence, submissiveness, passivity, and so on" to the point where "it will create a work situation which requires immature, rather than mature, participants" (p. 151). The span of control needed to be balanced between the tasks involved and the personalities of the followers.

Conclusions were drawn after reviewing the existing thoughts on organizational structures and personality. Argyris (1987) asserted:

> if the principles of formal organization are used as ideally defined [by prior research] , then the employees will tend to work in an environment where (1) they are provided minimal control over their work-a-day world, (2) they are expected to be passive, dependent, subordinate, (3) they are expected to have a short-time perspective, (4) they are induced to perfect and value the frequent use of a few superficial abilities, and (5) they are expected to produce under conditions leading to psychological failure (p. 151).

These characteristics were similar to the ones found in children. Incongruency thus existed in organizations that created these conditions. Argyris (1987) further elaborated by stating that "formal organizations are willing to pay high wages and provide adequate seniority if mature adults will, for eight hours a day, behave in a less mature manner" and it gets worse the more maturity employees possess, the more closely they're supervised, the lower a person is on the hierarchical structure, or as the tasks become more specialized (p. 151).

Argyris focused on the interaction between the individual's personality and the organizational structure. It was his belief that the negative aspects, such as failure to accomplish goals and objectives, follower frustration, and poor leader-follower relationships, that organizations face were the result of inconsistencies between follower personality and organizational goals and objectives. Organizational designers need to be aware of this conflict when they set out to design a new or redesign an existing organizational structure.

*Rensis Likert.*

Rensis Likert (1987) provided the rationale for the linking of leadership and followership styles, suggested that satisfaction drove performance, and that followers should be allowed to work to their ability. His research focused on the comparison between high- and low-producing managers. The dynamic external environment was also a factor in determining how the organization and its members interacted. The result of his analysis was a theory of management and organization that he felt could be applied to any organization.

Likert (1987) suggested that the high-producing managers he studied deviated from their use of traditional organizational theories in such as way as to produce organizations characterized by highly motivated followers (p. 218). The favorable follower attitudes were the result of the leader addressing the follower's ego, security, creativity, and economic motives. The leader also fostered trust by communicating effectively, being sensitive to follower needs, using performance goals to provide guidance, and allowing them to participate in making decisions. The result was an organization that "consists of a tightly knit, effectively functioning social system" (Likert, 1987, p. 219).

Likert identified characteristics of leaders who were able to create these types of organizations. The leader approached his role in a supportive and friendly manner that was consistent with the followers' perception of it. Confidence in follower ability "leads [the leader] to have high expectations as to their level of performance" which "is fundamentally a supportive rather than a critical or hostile relationship" (Likert, 1987, p. 221). The leader provided adequate training to followers and helped those with substandard performance to improve by providing additional training and support and instilling confidence. The final characteristic involved utilizing participation and group-leadership practices to build "subordinates into a working team with high group loyalty" (Likert, 1987, p. 221).

The characteristics of the leader and followers in high-producing organizations led Likert (1987) to develop a *"principle of supportive relationships"* that he defined as:

the leadership and other processes of the organization must be such as to ensure a maximum probability that in all interactions and all relationships with the organization each member will, in the light of his background, values, and expectations, view the experience as supportive and one which builds and maintains his sense of personal worth and importance (pp. 222-223).

The background, values, expectations, and experiences were what helped determine a person's personality and they affected leaders and followers in the same way. Likert (1987) suggested that personality and each one's perception of the surrounding situation was the basis for how leaders and followers reacted to each other and their environment (pp. 222-223).

A second aspect of Likert's supportive relationship theory was that the followers should view their tasks as difficult, important, and meaningful. This implied that the growth needs which were derived from each person's personality had to be satisfied by the key aspects of the tasks. Likert (1987) added that each follower's positive perception was "necessary if the individual [was] to achieve and maintain a sense of personal worth and importance" (p. 223). High-producing leaders who found follower dissatisfaction realized that it was important to redesign the tasks in order to bring about increased satisfaction.

The leader may or may not know how to determine if follower satisfaction was high or low. This could be accomplished by appropriate measurement instruments or by "development of work-group relationships, which not only facilitate but actually require, as part of the group building and maintenance functions, candid expressions by group members of their perceptions and reactions to the behavior of others" (Likert, 1987, p. 224). The effectiveness depended on the leader's ability to either choose and implement appropriate instruments or harness the results of group interaction.

Likert (1987) then added that "an organization will function best when its personnel function not as individuals but as members of highly effective work groups with high performance goals" (p. 224). The structure of the groups should be such that a link between each group existed. This link was a person who was a member with different roles in different groups. This meant that a follower in one group was a leader in a group that was lower in the hierarchical structure. When implemented correctly, there was a link from the top of the organization all the way to the bottom and back up again. This linking function enhanced the supportive relationship theory.

A key to the linking pin concept was that leaders in one group must be able to communicate with and influence their leader in the group in which they were a follower. Likert (1987) suggested that "to be effective in leading his own work group, a superior … needs to be skilled both as a supervisor and as a subordinate" (p. 233). The ineffectiveness became more profound for the organization the higher up the structure it existed therefore efforts to make sure that communication and influence were equivalent throughout was the focus of organizational designers.

A final aspect of Likert's principle was that the organization's objectives and the personalities of the followers were dynamic. External factors influence the organization's structure while each person's growth needs affect their satisfaction relevant to their tasks. The organization must be able to accommodate the changes in the external environment and make them fit with the needs of the followers in order to ensure that they are motivated and the organizational objectives are accomplished.

High-producing managers were ones that provided support, instilled confidence, and employed a participative leadership style in a continuous linking function from the bottom of the organization to the top. Likert felt that organizations became more productive as leadership styles progressed toward the participative end from the authoritarian end. The external forces in the organization's environment dictated that this leader must not only be able to change the structure as necessary but be able to do so in a way that was compatible with follower needs.

*David R. Frew.*

David R. Frew (1977, 1981, and 2002) developed a theory that different task structures required different leaders and followers, each person possessed both a leadership style and a followership style that were relatively stable over time, and that organizational effectiveness would be at its greatest when the structure and styles were similar. His theory was based on the belief that leadership and followership styles were derived from the personality of each individual and would only change as a result of a significant event in the short run or forces that elicit gradual change over time. His work produced a set of measurement devices to determine the style of leaders and followers as well as the nature of the task environment.

Frew's research began as a way to predict leadership effectiveness and organizational success. He developed the Perceived Task Complexity (PTC) as an instrument to measure the task environment so that individuals could "develop an insight into the notion of task complexity" (Frew, 1981, p. 92). The results of his research suggested that low PTC jobs, which were simple and routine types, were best suited for autocratic leaders and followers while high PTC tasks, which were complex and unpredictable, were best suited for democratic leaders and followers.

It was felt that "a good deal of a supervisor's success at work was dependent upon the general level of acceptance of leadership by the staff" (Frew, 1977, p.91). Organizational success depended on the relative satisfaction a follower felt as a result of the fit between their tasks and leaders' styles with their own followership style. Every organizational member had a leadership style as well as a followership style and both were based on each person's personality. Frew (2002) felt that since personality was relatively stable over time it was an effort in futility to try to change a follower's

personality (personal interview, January 29, 2002).

Successful leaders were ones who were able to determine their styles, understand

the degree of complexity of the tasks, and an awareness of the follower styles. Frew

(1977) felt that "it doesn't make much sense to try to change our personal styles, but it is

very useful to be able to learn what they are and what that might lead to" with respect to

success (p. 93). He devised a set of instruments to measure the leadership and

followership styles and the complexity of the tasks. The instruments, known as the

Structural Followership Profile and the Structural Leadership Profile, measured the types

of followership and leadership styles respectively that each person possessed. The styles

of the leaders and followers were then compared with the task complexity to determine

the degree of fit. The implicit assumption was that when the leadership style,

followership style, and task environment were similar leaders and followers would be

most comfortable and satisfaction would be maximized.

Frew (1977) suggested that "both common sense and research experiences point

toward a few emergent principles of organizational effectiveness" that organizational

designers and leaders should employ (p. 97). The principles may be applied after the

measurement instruments have been filled out and analyzed. Leadership and

followership styles were derived from personality and were thus difficult to change,

especially over short time periods. An understanding of the interaction between the

styles and the environment and knowledge of the styles that exist allowed one to make

informed decisions about whether or not a particular leadership style would or would not

be effective. Frew (1977) felt that "leaders who naturally tend to operate with a broad

range of behavior patterns tend to be more successful and more comfortable" (p. 97).
There are also leaders who are not as comfortable working in a dynamic environment and
can only manage with patterns that are in a narrow band. Care should be taken to
understand the environment that leaders will operate in and properly select leaders who
can function in it. The same can be said for followers as they need to be properly
selected as well. Tasks that became more complex required leadership patterns that were
more democratic and as they move in that direction, "special care should be taken to staff
departments with democratic followers" (Frew, 1977, p. 97).

David Frew stated that leaders and followers each have a leadership and
followership style. How well the styles fit with each other and the degree of complexity
in the task environment determined the degree of satisfaction that existed at any given
time. The styles were based on personality and were relatively stable over time. A result
was that proper selection of both leaders and followers whose styles fit fairly well with
each other and the task environment resulted in increased satisfaction among
organizational members.

*Robert Tannenbaum and Warren H. Schmidt.*

Robert Tannenbaum and Warren H. Schmidt (1987) added some insight regarding
forces that affected the interaction between leaders, followers, and the organizational
structure. The interaction focused on the tradeoff between leader authority and the
degree of control exercised in a given situation. They also advocated a contingency or
situational approach to leadership that took an alternative view of the theories addressed
to this point.

Tannenbaum and Schmidt (1987) felt that "the problem of how the modern manager can be 'democratic' in his relations with subordinates and at the same time maintain the necessary authority and control in the organization for which he is responsible" was the impetus behind the development of their approach to leadership (p. 264). The realization was that conflict existed for a leader between making a decision and implementing it on his or her own or involving the followers in the process.

They devised a continuum of leadership behaviors that, along with an understanding of the forces that surrounded leaders, served as a framework for leaders to help understand how to deal with the conflict and allow them to select appropriate behaviors based on the situation. The continuum contained a range of actions based on the degree of authority a leader used and the degree of freedom the followers possessed as a result of where the leader was on the continuum. The ends of the continuum were similar to continuums offered by other theorists as the extreme left represented a high degree of authority or control while the right side represented a low degree of leader control and a high degree of follower freedom. The styles that were between the two ends were a mixture of increasing degrees of follower freedom and decreasing leader control and vice versa. Tannenbaum and Schmidt (1987) added that "at the extreme left of the range, the emphasis is on the manager – on what *he* is interested in, how *he* see things, how *he* feels about" the followers in the organization while on the right side the emphasis is on "the subordinates - on what *they* are interested in, how *they* see things, how *they* feel about" the managers (p. 268).

Tannenbaum and Schmidt (1987) suggested that a few issues that arose had to be considered when their view of leadership was analyzed (p. 268). There was concern that leaders who delegated to their followers would be viewed as relinquishing responsibility. Tannenbaum and Schmidt (1987) felt that leaders were held responsible by their superiors and that they could only delegate freedom to the extent that they themselves had freedom from their superiors; they thus assumed risks when they delegated, (p. 268).

Participation with followers after a leader delegated to them was another concern of leaders at the time. Leaders were uncertain whether they should not get involved with the decision making or be an active member of the process. Tannenbaum and Schmidt (1987) thought that there were instances where the leader should be involved and in instances when that was necessary he or she "should function as an additional member of the group" yet keep in mind that "it is important that he indicate clearly to the group that he sees himself in a *member* role rather than in an authority role" (p. 268). When this was done the members benefited from the additional ideas that a leader brought to bear on a problem.

A third consideration was the importance that a group be able to recognize the leadership behavior utilized by the leader. Tannenbaum and Schmidt (1987) suggested that "it makes a great deal of difference" because a good deal of the relationship problems between leaders and followers resulted because the leader failed to clarify how he or she planned to use authority (p. 268). This was particularly a problem when a leader tried to conceal his or her true intentions such as when a decision was to be made by the leader yet follower buy-in was important to implementation. Some leaders tried to get the followers to believe that the actual decision was their idea. Such a tactic was risky so the better approach was for the leader to be honest and clarify the role that followers are to take in decision making (Tannenbaum and Schmidt, 1987, p. 268).

Tannenbaum and Schmidt (1987) also cautioned leaders to be careful not to try and determine how democratic they were by counting the number of decisions the followers make (p. 269). This quantitative approach to leadership was an extension of the growth in the field of management science. Tannenbaum and Schmidt (1987) felt that the "sheer *number* of decisions is not an accurate index of the amount of freedom that a subordinate group enjoys" rather it is "the *significance* of the decisions which the boss entrusts to his subordinates" (p. 269). This implied that a decision as to employee parking for instance was not as important as decisions that affected how a given task was performed.

There were many factors that influenced how a leader chose to behave in a given situation. Tannenbaum and Schmidt (1987) stated that forces in the manager, forces in the subordinate, and forces in the situation were of greater importance than the rest and varied in strength, but "the manager who is sensitive to them can better assess the problems which face him and determine which mode of leadership behavior is most appropriate for him" (p. 269).

Forces in a manager contributed to the choices he or she made when a problem or task was encountered. A leader's personality influenced his or her behavior in any given situation (Tannenbaum and Schmidt, 1987, P. 269). This implied that factors that determine personality such as background and accumulated knowledge and experience are linked to the behavior of the leaders. Tannenbaum and Schmidt (1987) included a value system, a leader's confidence in his or her subordinates, his or her leadership inclinations, and a "tolerance for ambiguity" (p. 269-70). A person's background, knowledge, and experiences drive personality, which shapes the value system. The value system, with respect to this theory, focused on the beliefs that a leader possessed regarding how much decision making followers should ideally be allowed to exercise. The strength of this belief helped determine where on the continuum the leader would exercise control.

The leader's confidence in subordinates determined how much control he or she was willing to give up. Confidence in followers and degree of control were reciprocal as the more confidence leaders had in followers the less degree of control exercised and vice versa.

Tannenbaum and Schmidt (1987) believed that "there are some managers who seem to function more comfortably and naturally as highly directive leaders" while "other managers seem to operate more comfortably in a team role" (p. 270). This was an indirect way of agreeing with other theorist's suggestions that personalities were relatively stable and that they influenced behavior so one would expect that a leader would be more comfortable in a role suited for their given personality.

A fourth factor that affected the forces in a manager was a "tolerance for ambiguity" that resulted when leaders release control over decision making to followers thus resulting in a reduction of predictability on the part of the leader with respect to outcomes of the selected decisions (Tannenbaum and Schmidt, 1987, p.270). The level of uncertainty that leaders will tolerate varies greatly and will determine how much control one releases to the subordinates.

A leader needed to be aware of the forces in subordinates that affected their behavior when it came to deciding on the proper degree of control to exercise. Tannenbaum and Schmidt (1987) added that a leader "will want to remember that each employee, like himself, is influenced by many personality variables" and that "each subordinate has a set of expectations about how the boss should act" (p. 270).

The degree of control that a leader needed to exercise over followers was reduced when the subordinates possessed a high need for independence, were ready and able to take responsibility for decision making, and had a high "tolerance for ambiguity" (Tannenbaum and Schmidt, 1987, p. 270). These aspects were related to the follower's personality and were relatively stable over time. Other factors were the follower's interest in the problem or task and whether or not they understand and agree with the goals and objectives of the organization.

A final and critical factor of the forces in the subordinate was whether over time they have experienced decision making situations. Tannenbaum and Schmidt (1987) claimed that:

> persons who have come to expect strong leadership and are then suddenly confronted with the request to share more fully in decision making are often upset by this new experience. On the other hand, persons who have enjoyed a considerable amount of freedom resent the boss who begins to make all the decisions himself (p. 270).

Leaders must be aware of how the degree of control that they have exercised over time, especially when they feel the need to alter it. An important consideration would be to make sure that the change is really necessary, clearly explained to the followers, and done only after careful analysis of all factors.

The third factor that influences how a leader will select a behavior was the forces in the situation. Tannenbaum and Schmidt (1987) stated that "among the more critical environmental pressure that surround [a leader] are those which stem from the organization, the work group, the nature of the problem and the pressures of time" (p.271).

The type or structure of the organization was concerned with the formal aspects such as job descriptions, policies and procedures, and organizational flow charts. The informal aspect was primarily related to the unofficial organizational culture that existed among all members. Tannenbaum and Schmidt (1987) added that "the amount of employee participation is influenced by such variables as the size of the working units, their geographical distribution, and the degree of inter- and intra-organizational security required to attain company goals" and that these may significantly impair the "manager's ability to function flexibly on the continuum" (p. 271).

Group effectiveness was based on the dynamics of the group itself. Factors like the experience followers have had working in groups, their ability to cooperate, whether members have similar backgrounds and interests, and the degree of confidence the group has in its ability to accomplish tasks affected this aspect of the forces in the situation (Tannenbaum and Schmidt, 1987, p. 271-272).

The nature of the problem was concerned with the degree of complexity that was required to understand and solve it. Tannenbaum and Schmidt (1987) stated that "the key question to ask, of course, is 'Have I heard the ideas of everyone who has the necessary knowledge to make a significant contribution to the solution of this problem?'" (p. 272). There may be times when a complex problem required a leader to seek the input of the followers because his or her knowledge was limited or he or she may have solved the problem if the followers lacked the knowledge and he or she possessed it. Either way it was important for leaders to consider these aspects of the problem before deciding on how much control to keep or release.

The pressure of time was the fourth aspect of the forces in the situation. Tannenbaum and Schmidt (1987) felt that the more a leader "feels the need for an immediate decision, the more difficult it is to involve other people" (p. 272). Firms that experienced fast changing environments or sudden problems may at times have required one person to act as quickly as possible because groups may take longer to reach a consensus.

These three forces, in the manager, in the subordinate, and in the situation, influenced a leader when he or she needed to choose a given behavior. The successful leaders, according to this aspect of the theory, were those who were aware of the influences of each factor and how they determined which behavior was appropriate.

Thus far, the theory focused on the relative short-term. Tannenbaum and Schmidt (1987) suggested that leaders employed the above strategy when dealing with problems that were pressing or were short-term in nature and because of this a leader's "choice of a leadership pattern is usually limited" (p.272). Long-term problems or planning removed some of the emphasis on the above forces because a leader had some control over them in this time frame. Tannenbaum and Schmidt (1987) added that a leader "can, for example, gain new insights or skills for himself, supply training for individual subordinates, and provide participative experiences for his employee group" (p. 273).

The theory that Tannenbaum and Schmidt put forth has a couple of contradictions within it. There is an apparent contradiction to the belief that leaders may move back and forth along the continuum of behaviors or styles yet the authors indirectly implied that subordinates have relatively stable personalities and styles when considering the forces in the subordinate. If personalities are relatively stable, then they are for both leaders and followers not just for one group. In addition, followers are diverse in personality in any given group and all may not move in the same direction at the same time in a given situation so to hold one group, followers, constant and the not the other, leaders, was a contradiction since the behavior of both is influenced by personality. Tannenbaum and Schmidt correctly acknowledged that problems occurred when a leader changed his or her style after the followers were used to or learned a given leader style. Again – and this is very important - this implied that leaders change styles while followers usually do not which may lead to follower frustration and or resentment of the leader.

The second contradiction was based on the potential sub-optimal actions by the followers when a style changes after they are used to a given one. These actions "should not keep the manager from making a continuing effort to confront his subordinates with the challenge of freedom" (Tannenbaum and Schmidt, 1987, p. 273). If the followers reacted in a negative manner, it may not be ideal to continually try to force freedom on them, especially if their personality did not allow them to operate under a different leadership style. Indeed, Tannenbaum and Schmidt (1987) acknowledged as much when they stated in their theory that "to provide the individual or the group with greater freedom than they are ready for at any given time may very well tend to generate anxieties and therefore inhibit rather than facilitate the attainment of desired objectives" (p. 273). The rest of the theory has some aspects that add to the alternate contingency view that leadership styles are relatively stable on the continuum

The leader, according to Tannenbaum and Schmidt, was one who was aware of the forces that helped him or her determine which behavior or style should be employed from those available on the boss- and subordinate-centered continuum. He or she was also aware that over the long-term more control was available over these forces so that the goals and objectives of the organization could be better met. This contingency approach to leadership was prevalent among those who felt that a leader may move relatively easily back and forth across the continuum of styles.

*Thomas Hobbes.*

Thomas Hobbes, born in England in 1588, was considered an empiricist who, among other things, discussed the rights of individuals and society. The motion of bodies and mathematics with their emphasis on cause and effect was an area that Hobbes preferred to utilize when he attempted to explain things but "as far as the remote basis of philosophical knowledge is concerned, Hobbes is an empiricist" (Copleston, 1959, p. 3). The cause and effect of individuals in society was what Hobbes observed as he developed his work on universal rights and government.

Hobbes, in Copleston (1959), believed that every thing that existed was the result of some motion or cause (p. 25). Human beings were no different and it was suggested that passions were the driving force behind human actions. Each person possessed his or her own passions which gave society "a multiplicity of human beings, each driven by his passions .... which determine for him what is good and what is evil" (Copleston, 1959, p. 31). It was the consequences or effects of these passions that were the driving force of society's development. Morality was defined by these people on an individual basis.

Each individual's diverse passions led to problems when they encountered other's passions. Hobbes claimed that "every individual seeks his own conservation and his own delectation leads to competition and mistrust of others" that he referred to as "the natural state of war" where each person "is dependent for his security on his own strength and his own wits" (Copleston, 1959, pp. 32-33). The only way to survive was to be crafty, strong, or to join together with others in a group that each member could benefit. In the absence of this binding together for mutual benefits "there are no objective moral distinctions" and "the notions of right and wrong, justice and injustice, have no place" (Copleston, 1959, p. 33). Hobbes (in Copleston, 1959) added that in this state each person was "judge of good and evil actions" and that the only wrong was "whatsoever a man does against his conscience" (p. 43).

The same passions that created the mistrust in others also brought about an ideal solution. Because individuals were self-interested there was a strong desire on their part to preserve what they possessed. Copleston (1959) stated that Hobbes believed "the rational pursuit of self-preservation is what leads men to form commonwealths or states" (p. 35). This commonwealth was founded on the basis of a contract or covenant. Individuals entered into an agreement, defined by Hobbes as "the mutual transferring of right," and were thus held to performance of their defined obligations. Copleston (1959) added that Hobbes felt the law of the contract was "the fountain of justice" and that "when a covenant is made, to break it is unjust" (p. 37). Once formed the contract then became a determinant of what was right and wrong with respect to the items in the contract.

The most important aspect then of this commonwealth agreement was that once entered into failure to comply with the agreement was an injustice to the organization formed from it. Until a contract was entered into there was no injustice. The obligation of individuals to perform their contractual responsibilities was binding on the conscious because "man's desire for security dictates that he should ... desire that the laws should be observed" (Copleston, 1959, p. 37). Once again the passions of man interfere and may not be sufficient or strong enough to bring about performance. This led Hobbes to state "covenants, without the sword, are but words, and of no strength to secure a man at all" (Copleston, 1959, p. 38).

The final matter pertaining to commonwealths and the contracts that bound and determined right and wrong was just exactly what rights were given up in exchange for the protection offered. Copleston (1959) stated that Hobbes believed "it is clear that in no commonwealth are all actions regulated by law ... [and] hence subjects enjoy liberty in these matters" (p. 45).

Hobbes felt that individuals left to their own desires and passions would exist in nature in a state of war. In this state each person determined what was right or wrong for him or her irrespective of others. The state of war thus made it necessary that individuals, for self-preservation, enter into binding agreements with others. As part of the agreement each person was bound both consciously and legally to perform according to the agreement. The contract thus defined right and wrong along with justice and injustice with respect to rights given up by the individuals. All other rights not given up remained with the individuals who were thus able to continue defining right and wrong with respect to those items.

*John Locke.*

John Locke (1988) was a political and philosophical writer who published his most famous work, *Two Treatises of Government,* in 1698. The primary assertion was that all people were free based on the Law of Nature and once ownership of property began in a society a need for laws and governance became necessary in order for protection to be established. When members of an organization voluntarily gave up some of their rights to a leader or group of leaders in exchange for protection the leader had an obligation to act in the best interests of the followers. A leader's failure to use power properly provided the followers with the right to initiate a change in the government.

The basis of Locke's theory was the Law of Nature, which in turn was based on reason. The Law of Nature stated that all persons were equal and independent, no one had the right to harm another person's life, liberty, or property, no one had power over another, and violations of said law gave the violated the right to punish the transgressor (Locke, 1988, pp. 269-272). Part of this statement may have resulted from his belief that divine law demands it. Locke stated:

> That God has given a rule whereby men should govern themselves, I think there is
>
> nobody so brutish to deny. He has a right to do it, we are his creatures: he has
>
> goodness and wisdom to direct our actions to that which is best; and he has power
>
> to enforce it by rewards and punishment, of infinite weight and duration in
>
> another life: for nobody can take it our of his hands. This is the only true
>
> touchstone of moral rectitude" (Copleston, 1959, p. 125).

Yet as people began to congregate together their interests collided. Locke (1988) asserted that the enjoyment of one's rights was "uncertain, and constantly exposed to the

Invasion of others" (p. 350). Some rights were then given up by a society's members in exchange for protection of their property. Locke felt this was done "for the mutual preservation of their lives, liberties, and estates, which I call by the general name, property" (Copleston, 1959, p. 132). Property could also be defined as the value added to a product or service as a result of one's labor.

The Law of Nature implied that there were no primary set of man-made morally right and wrong actions. When rights were given up the governing bodies and their guiding laws relative to the rights then became the code of morally correct and incorrect behaviors. Copleston (1959) felt that Locke defined morally good acts as "the conformity of our voluntary actions to some law" and wrong acts as "the disagreement of our voluntary actions with some law" (p. 124). The laws were utilitarian in nature in that they were designed for the good of all and applied to everyone the same way. The laws themselves were backed by sanctions that were utilized by those who possessed the power to govern. When laws conflicted with each other, "divine law is the ultimate criterion, in relation to which voluntary actions are called morally good or morally evil" (Copleston, 1959, p. 125).

Three types of power existed according to Locke. Paternal power was that which was exercised over those individuals who were unable to manage their own property and rights (Locke, 1988, p. 384). Children lacked the capacity to look after their rights so someone was needed to act on behalf of them. Once they achieved a certain level of competence the paternal power was removed. Locke (1988) added that "parents" were responsible to "inform the Mind, and govern the Actions of their yet ignorant Nonage, till Reason shall take its place, and ease them out of that Trouble" (p. 306). Individuals who were not children and still lacked the competence required someone to look after them but to do so in a fiduciary manner.

Political power was that power voluntarily given up by persons who possessed property and rights under the Law of Nature to the governing organizational body, whether it took the form of one individual or many. The power wielded by the leader was guided by explicit or implicit rules in a contractual arrangement and could be removed by the followers if the contract was broken. Locke (1988) said that this transfer of rights "*puts Men* out of a State of Nature and *into* that of a *Commonwealth*" which, through its legislative apparatus, enacts "Laws for him as the publick good of the Society shall require" (p. 325). Each individual who agreed to the transfer was obliged to submit to the actions the government carried out as long as they were within the context of the social contract that was derived from the majority.

Despotic power was wielded over those individuals who lacked any property or rights. Locke (1988) asserted that this type of power was "an Absolute, Arbitrary Power one Man has over another, to take away, his Life, whenever he pleases" and that it was not derived from nature because there was a lack of "distinction between one Man and another" (p. 382). The only positive thing that could be said about despotic power was that all governed individuals were treated equally. That equal treatment, however, was generally oppressive in nature.

Failure of the governing person or body to follow the established laws set forth in the contract was morally wrong and thus entitled the society's members to change the person or body. This was similar to Hobbes belief that the individuals had a moral right to obey the laws only so long as the administrator of the contract's laws wielded them as indicated. Copleston (1959) added that Locke believed "if the holder of supreme executive power abandons or neglects his charge so that the laws cannot be enforced, government is effectually dissolved" and the result is that "rebellion is justified" (p. 138).

The span of government styles in Locke's theory ranged from despotic or absolute power on one end of a spectrum to the State of Nature or extreme democracy on the other end. The despotic end was characterized by a lack or absence of property and rights along with laws that were enacted and carried out solely at the whim of the governing body. Locke stated that in this instance "where there is no property there is no injustice" (Copleston, 1959, p. 126). The State of Nature end was characterized by the presence of property, all rights were reserved for each individual except in the case of incompetence, and there were no laws to be followed. The area between both ends encompassed a mixture of both forms. Locke would most likely have preferred an organization that would be close to the State of Nature end of the continuum but only far enough away to just protect the property and rights of the commonwealth. Individuals were willing to move back on the continuum from the State of Nature only enough as necessary because "no rational Creature can be supposed to change his condition with an intention to be worse" (Locke, 1988, p. 353). Large movements from the State of Nature end toward the despotic end could only be accomplished by a usurpation of power by another or through tyranny of the commonwealth members (Locke, 198, pp. 398-399). The means of usurpation or tyranny were usually by some form of force. The despotic type of government "which by some Men is counted the only Government in the World, is indeed *inconsistent with Civil Society*, and so can be no Form of Civil Government at all" (Locke, 1988, p.326).

John Locke developed a theory of human behavior and government that adequately explained the reasons why individuals gave up rights and the role of leaders and followers in organizations, in this case government. The result of interaction between free individuals created anxiety among them regarding protection of their property that could only be rectified by the introduction of a responsible government organized and operated through the use of a contract or covenant. Locke favored highly democratic governments but it was possible that any form was ideal depending on the level of anxiety of the individuals and how much property and rights they were willing to give up in exchange for peace of mind.

*Common theme.*

The common theme among the researchers was the existence of a continuum for leadership and followership styles and the task environment ranging from simple, authoritarian, or autocratic to complex, participative, or democratic. The research provided the authority on which to base my assertion.

Max Weber's theory provided a few items for leaders, followers, and the organizational structure. Rules and procedures should be based on consensus, expediency, and relevancy to the tasks to be completed and could be applied to any type of organization, whether it takes the form of an autocracy, a democracy, or somewhere in the middle. The rules should be abstract enough to allow flexibility and should not be shaped to a particular person. The leaders are selected for their positions based on their qualifications to fill the office. Followers obey the rules and procedures and not individuals which provides a level field for all and thus equality amongst them. A grievance process must be in place to allow for conflict resolution in the event that problems of accountability arise. The extreme realization of this equality is democracy.

Mary Parker Follett augmented leadership aspects to this work. A leader should have knowledge of the tasks involved, the ability to look a the whole picture and see the relevancy between the various factors as they are affected by dynamic external forces, and should delegate authority to the followers by providing the competent ones with adequate training. The followers then have some responsibility for their actions up to their competency level with respect to the tasks and should be able to help the leader lead.

Taylor's Scientific Management added aspects to the work primarily related to structure but also some insight in leaders and followers that apply to all types of organizations no matter where they are on the autocratic-democratic continuum. The structure of tasks should be based on relevant information required to do the tasks and nothing more. The implementation of a new process or structure in an existing organization should consider the initial resistance that may materialize as followers may be reluctant to change. Followers then should be selected based on how well they fit the tasks. Leaders and followers are made responsible to accomplish the goals and objectives and the followers can hold the leaders accountable for their part. The level of satisfaction on the part of leaders and followers increases productivity and may be a result of a good fit between both of their styles with the task environment.

Douglas McGregor's Theory X and Theory Y dealt with leaders and followers. The range of styles is on a continuum that is autocratic or directive on the left end and democratic or participative on the right end. Followers are not passive and the leader's role is primarily to organize resources required to accomplish organizational goals and objectives. McGregor emphasized that leaders should organize resources in such a way that allows followers to satisfy their own needs. However, it is difficult to satisfy all needs of the followers due to the scarcity of resources and logistics so caution must be employed when attempting to do so.

Jay Lorsch offered insight into the design of an organization's structure regardless of where if should be on the continuum and suggested that there was no one best structure. Dynamic external forces, the tasks to be accomplished, and the characteristics of the people involved are the factors in designing new or modifying existing organizations. The external forces range from simple to complex and have varying degrees of certainty with respect to future outcomes. A conflict resolution process must also be designed into the structure in order to deal with any problems that may arise regarding interaction between leaders, followers, and the organization.

The work of Chris Argyris enhanced the work of this paper by providing understanding into interaction between followers and the structure. An individual's personality development begins at a passive and dependent state and progresses toward an active and independent state. The development can range from an erratic short term to a more stable long term time frame. Each individual will progress along the dependent-independent continuum to some point somewhere between them. Some may not progress very far while others may progress to the far end of independence. The majority will fall somewhere in the middle. The task environment ranges from simple to complex tasks that determine the type of direction that followers need. Incongruencies between the follower's personality and an organization's task environment may lead to suboptimal performance. The organization then needs to be designed or redesigned with the followers' personality in mind.

Insight into the interaction between leaders and followers was provided by Rensis Likert. A person's growth needs are derived from their personality and achievement of the needs determines satisfaction. Each person's background, values, expectations, and experiences influence his or her personality and perception of their environment and affects both leaders and followers the same. Leaders and followers need to be linked together in some manner that provides a supportive relationship and allows accountability on both sides. This progresses from the lowest level of the organization to the top so that each leader is also a follower. Any changes to the organizational design that may be required due to external forces should consider how the growth needs of leaders and followers will be affected.

David Frew's theory was the basis for this work. Each person has both a leadership and followership style that fall on a continuum that ranges from autocratic to democratic types and are influenced by his or her personality that is relatively stable over time. Simplistic and stable task environments are best suited for autocratic types while complex and dynamic environments are best suited for democratic styles. The success of the organization hinges on the satisfaction that leaders and followers perceive as a result of the degree of fit between each other and the task environment. Since personalities are relatively stable over time it is futile to try to change a person's personality to fit the task environment so proper selection of leaders and followers is the way to ensure the fit.

Tannenbaum and Schmidt offered information relevant to this work in the area of leaders and followers. Personality influences behavior and is determined by a person's background, knowledge, tolerance for ambiguity, value system, and experiences. A person's personality is relatively stable. The value system determines how much power a leader uses and how much freedom a follower should have. The freedom that a leader gives a follower determines where the leader falls on a directive-participative continuum. The leader also determines how much freedom to give the followers based on the followers' experience, the leader's perception of the follower's need for independence and their ability to handle responsibility, and how much power a leader wants to retain.

There are other aspects of the research from Tannenbaum and Schmidt that facilitated this work. External forces affect how a leader will act at certain times. Sudden changes or big movements in a leader's style may upset followers as they are used to a given leader style. Time pressure is an added factor in how much freedom a leader gives followers as circumstances that require quick decisions may be hindered by increased follower involvement.

Thomas Hobbes asserted that notions of right and wrong were only defined by the social contract entered into by individuals. Any particular form of government was just as long as it was voluntarily entered into to by the followers and was implemented by the designated leaders as intended. When these conditions were met the social unit functioned as desired but when not adhered to as planned the mistrust would return and the individuals would revert back to the "natural state of war."

John Locke's theory of government furthered the assertion in this work. There are two ends of a continuum with respect to the amount of governance that an individual encounters. The despotic end is characterized by the absence of rights, property, and many rules that are enacted and executed at the sole discretion of the leader. The State of

Nature end of the continuum is characterized by the absence of any rules, all rights are reserved by each individual, and property is owned and protected by each person. Rights and property are voluntarily given up by individuals in a contractual agreement to a leader or governing body in exchange for protection of their property and or for a reduction in anxiety they may have over uncertainty that exists in the environment. The leader's contractual agreement requires that he or she exercise the power given in a manner that is consistent with what is best for the followers. Failure to do so entitles the followers to exercise a change in leaders. Followers will not move backward on the continuum away from the State of Nature unless they receive some greater benefit as they would never agree to worsen their condition. Large movements away from enjoyment of many rights against the will of the followers can only be done as a result of usurpation of power or tyranny.

It is my intent to determine whether the congruence of the styles and environment has any effect on the satisfaction of leaders and followers. If this turns out to be the case then it should not matter whether the congruence is at the autocratic and simplistic end of the continuum, in the central area, or at the democratic and complex end because their placement on the continuum will be optimum for each given instance. Notions of a right or wrong organizational structure may only be judged by the criteria of satisfaction of the participants.

The information gathered from the literature supports the assertions in this thesis and applies to any organizational form of any size whether it is a country, a public or private enterprise, or an informal civil group. It is my conjecture that a continuum exists for leader and follower styles that is similar to the continuum of the task environment.

The extreme left end of the leader continuums is based on a lack of participation, rights, and even property by followers, full exercise of power by the leader, and dependence by followers due to immaturity or lack of competence. The extreme right end of the leader continuum is based on full participation by followers in decisions, many rights, full ownership of property, and independence of the followers due to maturity or complete competence. There are a variety of styles in between the two ends that are a mixture of or tradeoff between the two opposing styles. The follower continuum is similar in structure to the leader continuum but exists because each person has both a leadership and followership style.

The task continuum has two ends that line up with the leader and follower continuums. The extreme left end of the continuum is characterized by a few and simple tasks, a stable environment, and a high degree of certainty. A leader or follower operates best and is most comfortable in this environment if each of his or her styles is autocratic and non-participative. The extreme right end of the continuum is characterized by many complex tasks, a highly dynamic environment, and a large degree of uncertainty. A leader or follower operates best and is most comfortable in this environment if each of his or her styles is democratic and participative. Satisfactory outcomes are the result of congruencies between leader and follower styles with the task environment. The closer the three are to each other the greater the satisfaction. This is important because the higher the satisfaction the greater the likelihood that the organizational goals and objectives will be accomplished.

Leader and follower styles are based on personality and are stable over time. The leader and follower styles will thus also be as stable and not likely to move much in either direction on the continuum over the short run.  Movements along the continuum will generally be in one direction, which is in the direction from the autocratic end toward the democratic end.  It is possible to move in the direction toward autocracy but it would either be only a slight movement which may be statistically insignificant or a large one that could only be brought about by massive disruption, use of force, or some other devastatingly traumatic and anxiety-producing situation that followers would gain some larger benefit over the loss of rights or property or leaders sense the need to impose greater control for the benefit of the followers.  Sudden changes in either direction will decrease satisfaction and result in an impediment to accomplishment of organizational goals and objectives.  It is possible that over the long term personalities and thus styles may change based on education, prolonged exposure to given circumstances, or tolerance for ambiguity that may move a leader or follower over a statistically significant distance on the continuum.

There is no ideal place on the continuum for the leaders, followers, and task environment to be for a given set of conditions as the most important factor is the congruency between each factor.  This implies that a very stable and simple environment with an autocratic leader who wielded power at his or her discretion would be perfect for immature and dependent followers just as a highly complex and rapidly changing environment with mature and independent followers sharing power with a democratic leader would.  Both types would have satisfied organizational members accomplishing their goals and objectives.

All aspects of an organization should be designed to accomplish the goals and objectives set out by the owners, whether the owners are citizens of a social organization or stockholders in a private enterprise. Organizations need to consider the external forces that will affect it over the expected life span. A changing environment may require a redesign of existing organizations or dissolution if the organization is non-governmental in nature. Rules, policies, and procedures should be designed only to accomplish the goals and objectives and should be related only to the tasks necessary to do so. Once tasks are designed proper selection of leaders and followers is essential except in the case of countries where followers are a given. Authority is given to leaders only to accomplish the tasks and follower involvement in the organizational compact, as part of their agreement to belong, is to adhere to the rules not the leader. A conflict resolution mechanism should be designed into the structure to ensure that problems are solved in the most efficient and effective manner. Extreme autocracies have leaders who may also be the owners and make the rules. Instances like this are the only exceptions where the organizational owner also creates the laws, enforces them, and is accountable to few or none.

Leaders have an obligation to act in the best interests of their followers. This is consistent with the congruency aspect because when the fit is close the leaders are allowing the followers to satisfy their needs. Even autocrats need to act in a fiduciary manner and may include satisfying such basic follower needs as protection, food, some type of education, and shelter. When the leaders fail to act in this manner followers are entitled to a change to bring about the ideal fit. The leader needs to be competent in terms of knowing how to run the organization. He or she should be capable of scanning the external environment and determining how present and future activities will affect the organization. The ability to steer the organization in a direction that is consistent with the organizational goals and objectives as well as the needs of the followers to survive in the future is a skill that is essential.

Time constraints may require that the leader temporarily assume more power than the followers would like or the leaders prefer in order to deal with pressing or emergency necessities. The leader must return to the original position after the situation has passed.

Followers have an obligation to actively provide feedback to the leaders about how satisfied they are and how they are interacting with the environment as well as holding the leaders accountable for their actions. Followers should be expected to assume as much responsibility as they are capable of and not any more that will hinder progress of the organization. They are also responsible to change the leadership if it does not address their needs, especially in the case of nations.

The main point is that no matter where on the autocratic-democratic continuum the congruence of the leader and follower styles with the organizational structure falls, satisfaction should be maximized if they are close. Organizational designers need to consider the congruence as well as external forces, the characteristics of leaders and followers, and the goals and objectives of the organization. Leaders and followers both have roles in an organization that involve the degree of responsibility each has, the rights and freedoms that each possesses, and the accountability of both parties in their combined pursuit of the desired outcomes. Careful consideration of these aspects by organizations should allow the successful completion of the goals and objectives by satisfied leaders and followers.

Chapter III – How to build an ideal salad

Analysis of the organizational structure, leadership style, and followership style will determine the congruence of each with the other two. The stability or elasticity of structure and styles for a given organization and period of time should also be a factor as any sudden movement, or attempt at movement, by any one of the three will produce incongruency. Does congruency between the leader and follower styles and the task environment have an effect on satisfaction? Analysis of the various factors over a period of time through a triangulation method I devised, referred to throughout as the Approximation Approach, helped determine the answer to this question and also attempt to quantify the satisfaction level of leaders and followers. The results of the congruency and satisfaction were plotted on a scatterplot and analyzed to determine whether the degree of congruency has any effect on the level of satisfaction of followers. The results add to the field of organizational leadership because it allows one to determine whether congruence has an effect and satisfaction is positively correlated with productivity then a set of conclusions can be derived that will assist organizational leaders in designing and leading any organization.

*Triangulation.* Triangulation as a means toward data quality is addressed as one element of the operative paradigm and is one of approximation that incorporates the methodologies set forth in Chapter II, supplemented by the use of hermeneutics. Denzin (in Robson, 2002) offered a number of types of research triangulation, of which data, methodological, and theory triangulation are used in this project. Data triangulation involves multiple sources while theory triangulation utilizes multiple theories to explain a phenomenon. The primary emphasis though in this study is methodological

triangulation. It is difficult to say that any of the qualitative approaches provide the most

useful knowledge, especially in the field of Organizational Behavior (OB), as they have

all been present in one form or the other throughout history.

Quantitative analysis offers a practical tool for those aspects that are directly

observable and quantifiable. The various aspects of OB generally have not been too

conducive to quantitative analyses but there may still be some aspects, such as those

aspects that can be ranked, ordered, or scaled in some manner that can be best viewed

from this perspective. It has been noted one must be careful with survey or interview

instruments as each, to some degree, "assumes knowledge of the relevant dimensions to

be studied" even if "it is not clear whether the initial item set is broad enough or relevant

to capture … critical themes" (Schein, 1990, p. 110). Despite this problem the analytical

approach is favored by many researchers as a tool with which to start the process.

Arbnor and Bjerke (1997) added that "the analytical approach … operates with a greater

number of a priori starting points (techniques) than the other approaches, which leads to

its operative paradigm being ready relatively *early* in a study" (p. 218).

The analytical approach for Frew (1981) in the form of the PTC instrument is a

good starting point for knowledge creation but there are also limitations when using

analytical analysis. Sir Isaac Newton (1962b) suggested that "since the quality of bodies

are only known to us by experiments, we are to hold for universal all such as universally

agree with experiments" that tend toward simplicity (p. 398). The simplicity of cause and

effect relationships as a result of experimentation or observations is something that many

researchers strive for in the process of explaining or understanding phenomena.

While simplicity may be one characteristic of the analytical approach empirical foundations is another. This too has its drawback as "an empirical judgment never exhibits strict and absolute, but only assumed and comparative universality" that is "an arbitrary extension of validity" (Kant, 1990, p. 2). Certainty in knowledge creation is not absolute because it is not possible to know everything that exists in entirety. Proponents of the analytical approach rely on a high degree of certainty for validity. A portion of the progression of analytical tools is built on the prior findings and experiences of other empirical findings which creates additional problems "for whence could our experience itself acquire certainty, if all the rules on which it depends were themselves empirical?" (Kant, 1990, p.3).

Analytical research tools that are based on prior research may not allow for near certainty in findings and their use may limit knowledge creation as researchers may place too much confidence in them. Kuhn (1996) elaborated on the progression of research findings as a "developmental process ... marked by an increase in articulation and specialization" (p. 172). Kant (1990) furthered this progression from the analytical or empirical perspective by stating that "the charm of widening the range of our knowledge is so great, that unless we are brought to a standstill by some evident contradiction, we hurry on undoubtingly in our course" (p. 5). Descartes (1999) agreed by stating "I learned not to believe anything too firmly about which I had been convinced by examples and custom alone" but found that researchers accepted things like established knowledge because "it is nearly always better to tolerate them rather than change them" (p. 11-13). Analytical tools provide a good starting point, like Frew's (1981) instrument, to begin research – or supplement it - because of their simplicity derived from empirical observations, the general acceptance of the established methods, and the validity that may

be present and apparent.  One is cautioned to be careful, though, to not put too much

emphasis on them because they may detract from further exploration of the phenomena

from other perspectives.

The systems or interpretivist approaches brings a more holistic view of

phenomena to the operative paradigm.  While some elements of objectivity remain in the

systems or interpretivist aspects they are primarily related to probabilistic characteristics

that were less certain than a purely analytical approach would require.  Newton (1962a)

felt that phenomena were better represented when researchers "distinguish [variables]

into absolute and relative, true and apparent, mathematical and common" (p. 6).  The

ability to understand stable structures as well as dynamic and nonregular processes on

more than one level of analysis improved the operative paradigm's validity as it is

another lens from which to view the reality of selected phenomena.  This provides

another lens from which to view the phenomena.  Descartes (1996) felt that it was

important in the knowledge creation process to "subdivide each of the problems that I

was about to examine into as many parts as would be possible and necessary to resolve

them better" (p. 16).

It is assumed that a majority of reality may be interpreted with the systems

approach in a manner consistent with what Giere (1995) suggested was near

approximations.  It is also a second step in the progression of knowledge creation from

simplistic to complex analysis that ultimately moves findings closer to certainty.

Since reality may never be able to be represented or understood by utilizing the

first two approaches, the actors or critical postmodernist approaches provides a third lens from which to view the reality of selected phenomena. Weber (in Gerth & Mills, 1973) felt that the "presuppositions" of science and the tools used "can only be *interpreted* with reference to its ultimate meaning, which we must reject or accept according to our ultimate position towards life" (p. 143). The construction of reality for a given phenomenon in the first two approaches may be too objective and thus may miss important characteristics. Newton (1962a) added that:

> it is indeed a matter of great difficulty to discover, and effectually to distinguish, the true motions of particular bodies from the apparent; because the parts of that immovable space, in which those motions are performed, do by no means come under the observation of our senses (p. 12).

The ability to engage in dialogue, immerse oneself in a culture, deconstruct the prevailing ideologies or accepted realities, or understand the realities by use of other senses gives triangulation as part of the operative paradigm the check on findings that a good model needs.

The actors check for the operative paradigm provides a means to ensure that nothing is missed or, as Gephart (n.d.) would have suggested from a critical postmodernist perspective, to uncover hidden meanings and interests or bring forth contradictions. Arbnor and Bjerke (1997) added that "what is commonly referred to as a 'lack of reliability' in social science results is, according to the actors approach, not lack but rather proof that the ultimate presumptions of the actors approach are relevant" (p. 231).

Triangulation of the three approaches offered by Scandura and Williams (2002) improves the ability to understand and explain phenomena. However, there is an apparent flaw in their view of triangulation.  Consider an equilateral triangle - equal sides and equal angles in Figure 1 that I refer to as the triangulation of approaches.

*Figure 1* - Triangulation of approaches

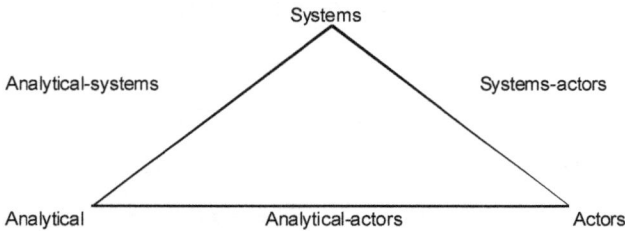

Systems

Analytical-systems                                                          Systems-actors

Analytical                              Analytical-actors                              Actors

This perspective has each approach an equal distance from each other.  The perspectives of each (the angles) are equal.  It would be rare for each perspective to carry unequal weight.  The existence of the analytical-systems and systems-actors blends has been discussed by Arbnor and Bjerke (1997).  The analytical-actors blend exists in a triangle for the very same reasons the others do but its characteristics are actually, or technically, a systems approach.  Since it is too broad and represents a tradeoff of the polar ends of a continuum, it (the side) is not equal to the other two and is thus a violation of the principles of a triangle.

If the triangle is an isosceles, obtuse, or some other triangle, it better reflects what triangulation was meant to be.  Each side's length varied with the perspectives (angles) used.  The presence of the analytical-actors side still must be considered even if it does not exist.  Since the perspectives exist on a continuum, which has a linear aspect to it, triangulation is an improper choice of models from which to explain the use of multiple lenses in knowledge creation. A better choice is one based on probability or approximation a view I shall call The Approximation Approach.

The Approximation Approach, in lieu of triangulation, of the operative paradigm is such that it provides a relatively high degree of reliability because it incorporates elements of quantitative analysis when needed, validity because it considers the nonregular aspects found in systems and relationships, and it is generalizable because the paradigm considers each situation or participant's perspective of reality which could not easily be done with the first two approaches. The analytical or positivist approach will be utilized to a small degree in most studies, the systems or interpretivist approach for the majority of analysis, and the actors or critical postmodernist approach to a smaller degree similar to the analytical or positivist approach. Figure 2 shows the probable distribution of use on the objective-subjective continuum and which forms the basis for this research's operative paradigm.

Figure 2 - Approximation of research distribution

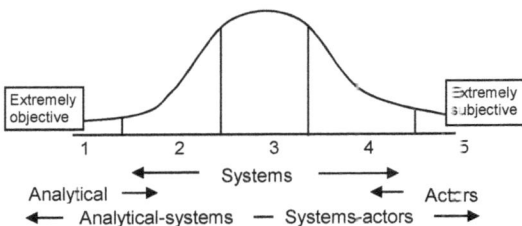

When considered from this perspective, the systems approach represents the broadest approach and is best suited to get as near to certainty as possible. It eliminates the analytical-actors requirement while still retaining the analytical-systems and systems-actors blends that Arbnor and Bjerke (1997) discussed  The analytical and actors perspectives are less likely to fully explain the congruencies alone but are still relevant and valid when used properly. The result is an element of the operative paradigm that one could utilize in many aspects of management, particularly OB, and ensures that it could be used in various cultures.

*How to survey the salad bar of leadership*

The analysis of task environment, leadership style, and followership style was conducted by sampling literature related to them over the course of 32 years of American history beginning in 1763 and continuing through 1794. 32 years was chosen as the time span because the country changed from a colonial dependent to an independent country, which would provide for variability in the environment and thus a way to see if satisfaction was present in many different types of environments. 1763 was chosen as the beginning because it was the year that America experienced its first strong desire for independence. The years between will be divided into two-year sets for analysis. The sets are defined as beginning with 1763-64 and labeled set 1 and ending in 1793-94 and labeled set 16. 1794 was chosen as the last decade because 3 congressional sessions and two presidential elections had passed giving an initial view of the relative short-term success of the government under the Constitution.

Each two-year set was analyzed in four parts. The task environment was analyzed by studying the prominent type of environment that existed throughout the period. It can range from a very simple and stable environment such as can be found in a minimally industrial and agrarian society. The other end of the range will be a highly complex and dynamic such as a largely industrial and urban society. Books on American history,

American history textbooks, biographies of individuals who lived during the time frame, as well as literary works that fairly represent the period will be read and used to determine the nature of the task environment.

The task environment can be described by the formal type of structure of the organization such as simple, complex, or somewhere in between the two. It can also be described as the collection of tasks and functions in an organization. Forces external to the organization should shape the objectives, which in turn define the structure. The structure then ultimately should determine how the tasks and functions of the organization are structured. The normal distribution of task complexity has a mean of 3.0 for the continuum of task complexity types that can be found when considering the task environment (Frew, 1981, p.88). The range is from super simple to very complex. The simple end of the continuum may also be labeled authoritarian or autocratic based on the minimum type of direction that is needed to get the basic amount of productivity accomplished when considering the tasks to be completed. The established standard deviations for this scale were 0.50 +/- one standard deviation, 1.00 +/- two standard deviations, and 2.00 +/- standard deviations. David R. Frew's (1981) Perceived Task Complexity (PTC) instrument, which can be found in *Personnel Administrator*, was used to code and determine the type of task structure for each period (p. 95-97).

Leadership style was analyzed by studying the leaders who were in influential positions or had the ability to influence a large percentage of the American public, either regionally or nationally, for each period. Autobiographies were the preferred source for obvious reasons as a means to determine leadership style but biographies were used as well. Some leaders, especially those who were influential during the years 1763-1775, were numerous or influential in only one region of the colonies but had crucial roles in the transition from dependence to independence. Complete autobiographies or biographies may not exist but the Library of Congress has short biographies on many of the leaders from years selected. Leaders who do not have sufficient biographical information were analyzed through historical texts or other forms of literature to glean personality attributes. Periods that contain more than one influential leader had their final leadership style calculated using weighted averages of the selected leaders based on the length of time each was influential as well as the magnitude or scope of their efforts.

An example of the calculation of weights for periods containing multiple influential leaders is illustrated in Table 1. Each leader for a period is placed into the table along with the time of influence out of 24 months and the scope of influence on a scale or one to three. The weights are calculated for each leader and multiplied by their final score in the leadership profile. The weighed scores are then added to give one final score for the leadership style for the given period.

**Table 1 - Calculation of weights for periods containing multiple influential leaders**

| Leader number, n | Leader name | Influence time, m (in months / 24) | Time factor, t (m/24*0.5) | Magnitude / Scope, s (from little - 1 - to great – 3) | Mag. / scope factor, f (s/3*0.5) | Sum of factors, x (t+f) | Weight, w (x / sum of x's) |
|---|---|---|---|---|---|---|---|
| 1 | Smith | 6 | 0.125 | 1 | 0.16666667 | 0.291667 | 0.155556 |
| 2 | Jones | 12 | 0.25 | 2 | 0.33333333 | 0.583333 | 0.311111 |
| 3 | Doe | 24 | 0.5 | 3 | 0.5 | 1 | 0.533333 |
| | | | | | Sum: | 1.875 | 1 |

n = leader number

m = months

t = time factor ((months / 24 total months) x 0.5)

s = magnitude or scope of influence on a scale of 1 (little) to 3 (great)

f = magnitude / scope factor ((s / 3) x 0.5)

x = sum of factors (t + f)

w = weight of each leader (x / sum of x's)

Leadership style can be described as the "idealized approach that a person would prefer to take to supervising" (Frew, 1977, p.91). The normal distribution of leadership style averages has an overall a mean of 3.0 for the continuum of leadership styles that can be found in an organizational environment (Frew, 1981, p. 88). The range is from extremely autocratic at the left end to extremely democratic at the right end of the continuum. Authoritarian may be substituted for autocratic just as participative may be substituted for democratic. The established standard deviations for this scale were 0.50 +/- one standard deviation, 1.00 +/- two standard deviations, and 2.00 +/- standard deviations. David R. Frew's (1977) Structural Leadership Profile instrument, located in *Personnel Journal*, was used to code and determine the leadership style of each President in the randomly selected decade (p. 94).

Followership style was analyzed by studying various types of literature from autobiographies, biographies, historical texts, novels from the selected, political economy and or philosophy for each selected decade. These were chosen, as they are reflections of the beliefs of followers during a given decade. The literature does not have to necessarily originate from the decade nor be exclusively American in origin but merely has to be the widely circulated and prevalent literature of the decade. The information gathered will be used to determine the followership style of the majority of citizens for each period analyzed.

Followership style can be described as "the kind of leadership patterns which would be preferred by an individual in his/her boss" (Frew, 1977, p. 91). The normal distribution of followership style averages has a mean of 3.0 for the continuum of followership styles that can be found in an organizational environment (Frew, 1981, p. 88). The range, as with leadership style, is from extremely autocratic at the left end to extremely democratic at the right end of the continuum. The calculated standard deviations were the same as the leadership scores. Authoritarian may be substituted for autocratic just as participative may be substituted for democratic. David R. Frew's (1977) Structural Followership Profile instrument, located in *Personnel Journal,* was used to code and determine the followership style of citizens in the randomly selected decade (p. 95).

Dr. Frew (1977) calculated the difference between followership and leadership scores to be 0.52 among all scores. The established standard deviations for the differences were set as 0.25 +/- one standard deviation, 0.75 +/- two standard deviations, and 1.25 +/- three standard deviations.

The degree of congruency between the three groups for each two-year period was calculated by taking the sum of the absolute values of differences of each score relative to the other two for the three categories and averaging them. Table 2 gives two examples of hypothetical task environments and styles. Once each period's task environment, leadership style, and followership style are determined the congruency will be calculated

in the manner shown. The minimum and maximum values of the degree of congruency

are 0.00 and 2.67, which represent complete congruency and the total lack of congruency

respectively. Example A in Table 2 depicts a total lack of congruency and thus has a low

degree of fit (congruency is 2.67) while Example B in Table 2 depicts a relatively high

degree of fit (congruency is 0.67).

**Table 2 – Calculation of congruence – absolute value of differences**

| Example A | Score | Calculation | Example B | Score | Calculation |
|---|---|---|---|---|---|
| Leadership style | 1 | $\mid 1\text{-}3 \mid = 2$ | Leadership style | 4 | $\mid 4\text{-}4 \mid = 0$ |
| | | $\mid 1\text{-}5 \mid = 4$ | | | $\mid 4\text{-}3 \mid = 1$ |
| Followership style | 3 | $\mid 3\text{-}1 \mid = 2$ | Followership style | 4 | $\mid 4\text{-}4 \mid = 0$ |
| | | $\mid 3\text{-}5 \mid = 2$ | | | $\mid 4\text{-}3 \mid = 1$ |
| Task environment | 5 | $\mid 5\text{-}1 \mid = 4$ | Task environment | 3 | $\mid 3\text{-}4 \mid = 1$ |
| | | $\mid 5\text{-}3 \mid = 2$ | | | $\mid 3\text{-}4 \mid = 1$ |
| | | $16 / 6 = 2.67$ | | | $4 / 6 = 0.67$ |

Social satisfaction was analyzed by examining an American almanac of history,

an American history textbook, and or a work of literature that fairly reflects the

satisfaction of each selected time frame. The almanac contains a list of significant events

that took place during each year, the history textbook will elaborate on significant events,

and the work of literature should provide some perspective of each selected year.

Social satisfaction can be described as the degree to which society feels that they are satisfied, complacent, or dissatisfied. The Social Satisfaction Instrument that I designed, located in Appendix A, measured this value. It uses a weighted average of two sections to attempt to quantify the degree of social satisfaction. The first section is qualitative in nature and focuses on the implied hope or despair that followers at the time would be expected to have based on conditions. The second section of the Social Satisfaction Instrument uses turnover in congress as an indication of citizen satisfaction with their government. The range of scores is from 0 to 4, with 0 representing extreme satisfaction and 4 representing extreme dissatisfaction. It was originally designed to be used for studying a wide range of American society since 1789. Since this research begins before Congress, as framed in the U.S. Constitution, the turnover in the Continental Congress will be used in the second section for the selected time periods from 1774 through 1789. Qualitative analysis will be substituted, in most cases, for the second section in the period from 1763 through 1774 and actual changeover in Congress from 1789 through 1794 will be used in the second section for the remaining periods. Figure 3 shows the possible distribution of satisfaction that could be expected, on average, during any given decade. The range is from extremely satisfied to extremely dissatisfied. The majority of the time (68%) it would be expected that society is complacent.

**Figure 3 - Social Satisfaction Distribution**

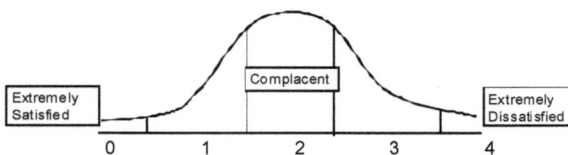

Once the congruence and social satisfaction values were determined for each period they were plotted on a scatterplot. Congruence is the independent variable and thus will be on the X-axis. Social satisfaction is the dependent variable and will be placed on the Y-axis. Thus Social Satisfaction (SS) = f (Congruence ( C )). Figure 4 shows the scatterplot that was used.

**Figure 4 - Scatterplot of congruence and misery**

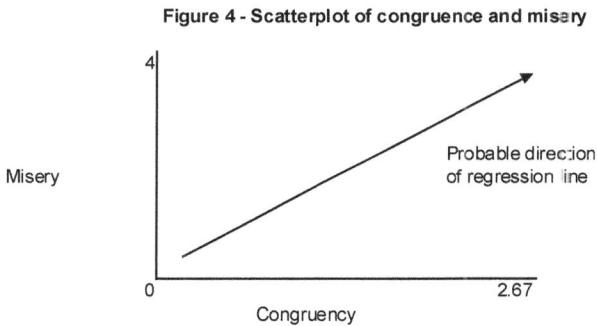

A linear regression calculation will be conducted after the selected time frames have been analyzed in order to provide a mathematical description of the association.

$$SS = a + b\ (C), \text{ where} \tag{1}$$

SS = Social Satisfaction

a = y-intercept

b = slope of regression line

C = Congruence of the task environment, leadership style, and followership style

A regression line will then be drawn in order to give a visual form of the association between the two variables. A Pearson Correlation (r) will be calculated to determine the measure of association between the variables.

r = ( sC / sSS) b, where                                                          (2)

r = Pearson Correlation

sC = standard deviation of Congruence

sSS = standard deviation of Social Satisfaction

b = slope of regression line

The Pearson Correlation ( r ) will then be squared to determine the proportional reduction in error, or coefficient of determination ($r^2$). This value will determine the strength of the linear association between C and SS.

Rival plausible explanations for the degree of social satisfaction that exists in each time frame could be chance, prosperity or economic success, geographic isolation of America, war, and culture. Chance effects will be controlled for by analyzing 16 time frames so that short-term events or rare occurrences should be noticeable as potential outliers and will be indicated during the review process. Prosperity or economic success cannot exist for an extended period of time because it is driven primarily by expectations of consumers and businesses that combined make up approximately 85% of Gross Domestic Product (GDP). If consumers and businesses are dissatisfied they will be frugal and not spend much. Geographic isolation is controlled for by focusing only on the colonies and early states. All thirteen colonies and states were relatively similar in terms of population distribution and commerce that was clustered near the ocean and its tributaries. War is such a significant event that it will affect the task environment, leadership style, and followership style at the same time and with a relatively equal force.

War's effects are controlled since it affects all in the same manner by potentially shifting them.

The results of the research may lead to conclusions for both new and existing organizations that leaders should consider when analyzing satisfaction in their environment. The decision-makers of an existing organization may want to change their organizational objectives, which would necessitate a change in the structure. Leader and follower styles may not match the new structure and thus they will need to be replaced or manipulated in some manner to shift them to approximately the same point on the continuum as the organization. Either of these tactics may be difficult as the labor pool may be limited, labor contracts may exist, or, in the case of a country, the followers may not be replaced except by inhumane means. The decision-maker may choose to leave the structure the same yet try to get leaders and followers to match the environment. This also may be difficult as it can take the form of manipulating or forcing the change or replacing the leaders and followers, which has the same implications as above.

A decision-maker may try to redesign an organization to be the same as the styles of leaders and followers. An example of this may shed some light on the implications of congruence and satisfaction. The American government that operated under the Articles of Confederation was considered unworkable by many after the Revolutionary War. A committee was convened to come up with new recommendations. New objectives were formed as manifested in the Preamble to the Constitution, a new government was formed from these objectives, and it operated as described in the Constitution. Satisfaction by leaders and followers may be a reason why it has survived this long.

New organizations have an easier time of increasing satisfaction. Decision-makers start by scanning the external environment and forming objectives based on what they want and how they will interact with the external environment. Once objectives are determined the organizational structure or task environment can be designed to optimally accomplish the objectives. Leaders may then be chosen based on the type of leadership style that will be most consistent with the environment. Followers are then selected based on the followership styles that they have. The result should be the optimum levels of satisfaction that may be obtained by addressing the congruency of all factors. The visual depiction of such satisfaction may be found by evaluating it relative to leadership styles as set up in Figure 5.

**Figure 5 - Possible satisfaction curve**

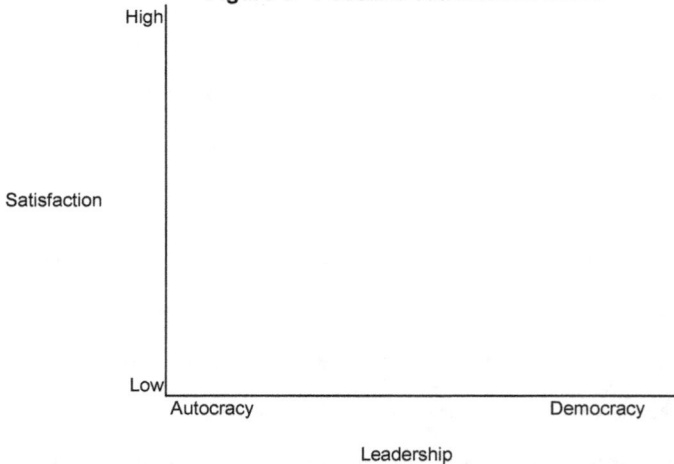

High

Satisfaction

Low

Autocracy                                                    Democracy

Leadership

Whatever the results of the research determine the field of leadership should be enriched, as any understanding of the dynamics that operate between the three should help leaders make better decisions and followers to understand more about their preferred style.

Anything that adds to the overall general satisfaction level of an organization should be a good thing.

Chapter IV – The real test – how good is it?

The results for the 16 sets of two-year periods were calculated utilizing the four quantitative instruments described in chapter III in conjunction with the Approximation Approach in mind. Attempts were made to apply the instruments to the American nation as an organization as best as possible. Those statements that did not properly fit with the circumstances, if applicable, were noted in the summary for each period. Each set was analyzed, a short narrative of significant events and people was given and the total results compiled at the end of the chapter.

*Set 1: 1763-1764.*

This set began with the signing of The Treaty of Paris which ended the Seven Years War between, among others, England and France. It was against this backdrop that the colonists expected to witness a resume to stability and prosperity. George III was firmly in power and Parliament proposed that a series of taxes be imposed on the colonists to cover the costs of defending them against the French and Indians during the war as well as some restrictions designed to clamp down on trade with other nations. The result was a series of acts by the colonists to counter this threat to their livelihood.

*Set 1 PTC and the task environment.* The Perceived Task Complexity Instrument was used to measure the degree of complexity prevalent in the colonies. Recall that the answers to the statements in this instrument ranged from strongly agree to strongly disagree. A more detailed analysis of how this and the other three instruments was employed in this set was discussed in order to provide some insight into the process. The degree of detail was not followed in subsequent sets for the sake of efficiency but the process remained the same.

Life was primarily rural in nature and the economy was based on exports. Bryant and Dethloff (1990) listed these exports items as "fur, timber, wood products, tobacco, bread, flour, rice, fish, and indigo" (pp. 38-39). Those in this basic environment would have answered statement one as strongly agreeing to a small number of clearly defined goals.

The majority of manufacturing took place in England with the finished products exported to the colonies. Bryant and Dethloff (1990) claimed that British merchants "possessed what the colonists lacked – capital, shipping, and established markets" but that "as the colonial economy matured the British mercantilist system tightened and became more constraining" (p. 39). Those in this period began to witness the early beginning of a change in the economy from rural to industrial. An example was that the manufacture of finished iron product, banned in the colonies since 1750, was also inefficient to do at the time but "the production of raw iron, which the colonies could do more efficiently" was on the rise (Bryant and Dethloff, 1990, p. 41). One would have agreed at this point that the environment was basically stable without much change.

The environmental uncertainty analysis began with The Royal Proclamation on October 7, 1763, where King George III declared that the new territories England received from France would be divided into four groups and governed by appointees of the crown and that:

any Lands beyond the Heads or Sources of any of the Rivers which fall into the

Atlantic Ocean from the West and North West, or upon any Lands whatever, which, not having been ceded to or purchased by Us as aforesaid, are reserved

to the said Indians, or any of them (King George III, 1763).

This act had forced all colonists who had moved into these areas to move out. It also

created uncertainty about future government because the crown was moving to exert

more influence on the colonists, who had in the past been mostly left to govern

themselves.

A second and more threatening act was The Sugar Act, also known as the

American Revenue Act and the Grenville Acts after British Chancellor of the Exchequer

George Grenville, who initially proposed the legislation. The Sugar Act was passed in

1764 by Parliament and imposed duties on imports into the colonies on items like sugar,

indigo, coffee, wines, silk, and other cloths. The stated reason was "for the better

securing and encouraging the trade of his Majesty's sugar colonies in American" and for

the revenue to be applied "towards defraying the experces [sic] of defending, protecting,

and securing the said colonies" while at the same time preventing illegal trade (British

Parliament, 1764). The duties infuriated colonists but the most infuriating aspect was the

establishment of a vice admiralty court in Halifax, Nova Scotia which had authority over

all of the American colonies. This court removed more of the colonies' authority over

themselves. Arthur Schlesinger (1993) added "The Sugar Act is notable in that it marks

the end of a strictly commercial British relationship with her American colonies and

initiates a policy of raising revenue" (p. 99).

The colonists perceived the actions of British government with disdain not only

because of The Sugar Act but the "corruption – corruption technically, in the adroit

manipulation of Parliament by a power-hungry ministry, and corruption generally, in the self-indulgence, effeminizing luxury, and gluttonous pursuit of gain" by others (Bailyn,

1992, p. 51). The Sugar Act and the corruption began to fuel resentment among the

literate and merchants and spreading to others that Raphael (2002) said "demonstrated the

instability of an American society still in the making" (p. 30). The analysis regarding

certainty would most likely be characterized as mixed.

The uncertainty that increased through the second year of the set was again due to

the actions of the British government to restrict the colonists' ability to make decisions

for themselves. The result was that many were unable to make predictions about what

the future held because events were rapidly changing the status quo. Colonists would

most likely have disagreed with the statements' assertions that the task environment

could be easily described or explained.

The score for this set was the average of the responses to the twelve statements in

the PTC instrument. The score was 2.83, which means that the environment was

somewhat simple to slightly mixed.

*Set 1 Structural Leadership Profile.*   The primary leader of this set was King

George III. The actions of his ministers and, to a lesser extent, the British Parliament

were primarily the result of his influence. His profile was analyzed by the Structural

Leadership Profile referenced in chapter III. The answers to the statements in the profile

ranged from strongly agree to strongly disagree.

A few of the statements in the instrument addressed the degree of control that a

leader expects from the followers. George III was a vain and self-assured person who

had little tolerance for incompetence. He came to the conclusion that "the longer he

lived, the more he realized how little trust could be reposed in most other men" (Hibbert,

1998, p. 27). The trust that he placed in individuals was limited to those who were very close to him and had been a part of his life for quite some time. Hibbert (1998) added that "it had to be said, though, that those who knew him best had observed in him an unfortunate lingering tendency to stress his own virtue when condemning the faults of others, as well as a disposition to harbour resentment" (p. 78). He would have strongly agreed to the statement related to followers explicitly adhering to his demands while he would have strongly disagreed to statement two that suggested tight control over followers does more harm than good. Statements seven and eight dealt with the degree of control and would have been answered with a strongly disagree (followers require minimum direction) and a strongly agree (followers require a strict leader). George III would have strongly agreed with statements thirteen through fifteen regarding the coordination of follower activities, the exercise of control, and the fact that there should be only one recognized leader. He would have disagreed with the instrument's suggestion that leaders should allow group consensus to develop action plans while he would have agreed with another statement and its implication that leaders are superior to their followers.

Additional statements were related to the responsibility that a leader felt he or she had for the results of any leader or follower actions. George III felt the need to control many facets of government as indicated in the previous paragraph and as such would have felt responsible for the results of any actions that he directed. He would have strongly agreed with another statement which asserted that any benefits to the organization were the result of the leader while he would have disagreed with the instrument's implication that a leader could not be blamed for failures or credited with successes. George III would have agreed with taking credit for successes but he may have attempted to place blame for failure on others since he felt that he was superior to followers.

George III believed that discipline was a necessary part of keeping followers in line. Hibbert (1998) stated that "one of the first acts of his reign was to issue a proclamation for the 'Encouragement of Piety and Virtue'" that had at its root the intention to "punish all manner of vice, profaneness, and immorality" that he encountered (p. 77). The punishment of wrongdoers stemmed from his religious upbringing and the influence of his closest friend and confidant Lord John Stuart, Earl of Bute. It was Bute's influence that led George III in 1762 to conclude that at times it was necessary "to call in bad men to govern bad men" (Hibbert, 1998, p. 91). George III would have disagreed with statement three and its assertion that discipline should be moderated. A strong disagreement with statement eleven would have been due to the fact that George III did not believe that discipline should be administered as a result of a democratic process. He would have strongly agreed with the instrument statement that a system of discipline be established and enforced while his willingness to have others enforce discipline for him weighed against a flexible discipline system would have prompted a mixed response to the statement regarding control and discipline.

The remaining statements focused on the delegation of authority and tasks to the organization's followers. George III was a micromanager who "gave careful attention … to almost all matters which were brought to his attention, trivial as well as important" (Hibbert, 1998, p. 72). This attention to detail and his mistrust of others shaped his belief of his role in government. Hibbert (1998) stated that George III "was well aware that theoretically nothing in either the Bill of Rights of 1689 or the 1701 Act of Settlement stood in the way declaring war, nominating peers, … and summoning or dissolving Parliament" (p. 76). George III would have had mixed feelings about statement four and the subdivision of tasks which it describes because, although he was a controlling individual, he did delegate some tasks, usually unpleasant, to subordinates. He would have also had mixed feelings about the role of a leader as one who assists in the leadership process rather than controls it, as question five stated, because he was willing to give up some aspects, usually unpleasant tasks, to trusted others primarily Bute. One statement also dealt with shared leadership but it indicated that at any one time there could be two or more leaders; George III would most certainly have disagreed with this. George III would have agreed with statement ten's assertion that leadership originate from the top with some exceptions. Finally, he would have strongly disagreed with the twelfth statement that followers could do their best if they determined their own actions.

The score for this set was the average of the responses to the twenty statements. The score was 1.80 which means that, according to the interpretations portion of the instrument, the "boss decides and announces decision, orientation" and is thus very autocratic.

*Set 1 Structural Followership Proflie.* The followers' thoughts and beliefs of this period and the responses that they would give if administered this instrument could best be analyzed by four individuals who were at the forefront of issues for this period. Samuel Adams, Patrick Henry, and James Otis with some insight added by Benjamin Franklin, provided the views of the majority of colonists at this time.

Religion still held a firm grip on society throughout the colonies but the signs of challenges to the system began to emerge, especially in Virginia where many began to resent the controlling influence of the religious leaders. A sermon in Connecticut on July 8, 1741 by Jonathon Edwards dealt with the need to be aware of one's sins because the wrath of God is strong and infinite. Edwards (1996) stated a prevalent theme among colonists that "people dread the wrath of kings, especially of dictators, who have people's lives and possessions totally under their power and can dispose of them at their mere will" (p. 19). Those who disobeyed the leaders could expect to suffer. The fear of leaders stuck with colonists in the early 1760s but the dread of suffering began to diminish as a series of actions against the established leaders, both religious and governmental, were brought about as the result of the injustices that many felt were being done to them. Bailyn (1992) added that:

"the threat of ministerial aggrandizement seemed particularly pressing and

realistic … in all but the charter colonies, held, and used, powers that in England

had been stripped from the crown in the settlement that followed the Glorious

Revolution as inappropriate to the government of a free people (p. 52).

The tone of intolerance toward tyranny was continued in this period by Patrick Henry, a lawyer from Virginia. Henry chose to defend the tobacco growers and the Virginia Act of 1758 in a suit by the clergy seeking to recover what they perceived to be a loss of revenue. It was during the course of his argument that he stated "a king and his people had a binding contract" and that whenever the contract was broken "a king ceased to be the father of his people and degenerated into a tyrant" (Langguth, 1988, p. 46). This was met with cries of treason from around the room but it marked the beginning of

Henry's stand against what he perceived to be overbearing and tyrannical government, in religion, the colonies, and Britain.

The passage of The Sugar Act was considered one of the most egregious acts of the period. Langguth (1988) suggested the colonists believed that "the idea of Britain levying taxes to raise money represented a shocking reversal of policy" because prior to its passage "taxes had been used only to regulate trade in ways that favored Britain" (p. 49). James Otis, a New England lawyer, published a pamphlet in 1764 that asserted the rights of the colonists with respect to the British government. Otis stated, among other things, that "supreme power should not be in the hands of *one* man" or office, that government's role was utilitarian in nature, its influence in everyday life should be minimal, and that it was up to the members of society to determine the form of government they wanted, whether it was to be a monarchy or a democracy (Otis, 1764). This was the first major statement of colonist's rights to be published. Taxation without colonial participation in the governing process, according to Otis, was tyrannical.

Benjamin Franklin believed that, in the case of levying taxes on the colonies, England should determine the colonists' share of responsibility for the war that just finished and let the colonies decide how to raise the money (Langguth, 1988, p. 51). This was a view of many at the time that the best way for the end to be met was to allow those responsible for it to determine how it should be done. Samuel Adams took the approach that Parliament simply had no right at all to tax the colonies without obtaining their approval first (Langguth, 1988, p. 49). His view, while not prevalent as of yet, was that participation by the colonists in Parliament, as proposed earlier by Benjamin Franklin, was a bad idea because "a handful of colonial members in the House of Commons would be swamped in every vote" because "with the delegates so far from home, instructions

sent from Boston would always be late and incomplete" while the Town Meetings that

were the cornerstone of many colonies "would be surrendering its authority" (p. 50).

Britain did not like Franklin's idea either as "it was judged to have too much of the

*democratic"* (Franklin, 1994, p. 171).

The passage of the Currency Act on April 19, 1764 prohibited the colonies from

issuing their own paper currency.  It specifically stated:

> no act, order, resolution, or vote of assembly, in any of his Majesty's colonies
>
> or plantations in America, shall be made, for creating or issuing any paper bills,
>
> or bills of credit of any kind or denomination whatsoever, declaring such paper
>
> bills, or bills of credit, to be legal tender in payment of any bargains, contracts,
>
> debts, dues, or demands whatsoever (British Parliament, 1764).

Schlesinger (1993) added that this act created "a common grievance uniting the more

commercial northern colonies with the agricultural southern colonies" because the effect

was deflationary and threatened "to destabilize the colonial economy" (p. 99).  Richard

Henry Lee (1764), a Virginia statesman, wrote in a letter to an unidentified person that

these types of taxes imposed without consent were "unreasonable impositions" that

would be akin to persons of reason giving up "liberty for slavery."  A Committee of

Correspondence was established on June 12, 1763 in Massachusetts to convey common

grievances among the other colonies.

Statements one through three and eight through ten were concerned with the

degree of control that followers expect in an organization.  Colonists would have answered with mixed feelings that actions be explicitly outlined, as statement one suggested, since they were arguing for local control. Statement two dealt with questioning the direction of leaders and the colonists would have disagreed that they should not do so as witnessed in the pamphlets and legal arguments of the period. They would have agreed with statement three's assertion that rigid rules and regulations created frustration as witnessed by the pamphlets and statements of leading individuals. Colonists would have disagreed with statements eight, nine, and ten which indicated that leaders should set rules and acknowledged that the leader was the leader and should not be challenged. The basis for these responses was the colonists' reactions to attempts at increased control by the clergy, to a limited extent, and the British government.

Statements four and fifteen focused on followers' views on discipline. The colonists would have agreed with statement four that they were capable of self-discipline. They would have had mixed feelings about expecting the leaders to give disciplinary guidelines, as in statement fifteen, because they still followed some of the established religious guidelines but were increasingly hesitant to accept them from a distant and unresponsive British government.

Responsibility was addressed in statements seven, twelve, and sixteen. Statements seven and twelve both considered whose fault it was when something was done that was wrong but was commanded by the leader. The colonists would have agreed with statement seven and disagreed with statement twelve as they were the same question worded differently. The arguments for more self-rule implied the acceptance of responsibility for their actions.

The remaining statements dealt with the delegation of authority. The colonists would have had mixed feelings about statements five, six, thirteen, and fourteen. Statements five and thirteen dealt with the amount of participation involved with daily activities while statements six and fourteen focused on the degree of deference given to the leader with respect to decision making. Statement eleven suggested that followers preferred general objectives and guidelines from which they could determine how to accomplish them. The colonists would have strongly agreed with this statement. The views of Adams, Henry, Otis and Franklin were the basis for these responses.

The score for this set was the average of the responses to the sixteen statements. The score was 3.44, which means that, according to the interpretations portion of the instrument, the follower style was a mixture of both autocratic and democratic styles. The fact that the score was 3.44 places the position almost into the moderately participative description.

The degree of congruence for this period was calculated utilizing the method in Table 2. The sum of the absolute values of differences was 6.56 while the average was 1.09.

*Set 1 Social Satisfaction Instrument.* The satisfaction of the majority of colonists can be viewed by the actions of the followers with respect to the five statements in section I of the instrument. Some of the actions have already been described in the previous sections and others will be offered in this section.

The response to statement one about the outlook for the future was two. The changing environment, in terms of the reduction in religious authority, the increased attempts to wrest control over local government by the British government, and Indian raids for those in the wilderness areas created a mixed outlook for the future. Bailyn (1992) elaborated on this environment by stating that:

> the epidemic evangelicalism of the mid-eighteenth century, had created challenges to the traditional notions of social stratification by generating the conviction that the ultimate quality of men was to be found elsewhere than in their external condition, and that a cosmic achievement lay within each man's grasp (p. 303).

The Proclamation of 1763, The Sugar Act, and The Currency Act were attempts to reign in the colonist's ability to rule themselves. Indian raids continued on settlers as they moved westward, sometimes in defiance of the Proclamation of 1763.

These same aspects also contributed to the response for statement two which addressed the satisfaction one experienced in life. The end of the Seven Years War gave a sense of relief in the early part of the period but began to give way to anxiety as the previously mentioned items came to the forefront of people's attention.

The colonists would have responded to statement three with a three, which is somewhat unresponsive. This was due to the fact that the British government was attempting to reign in the colonists' role in governing themselves. They would have given the same response, a three for little control, to statement four which looked at the degree of control they felt they had over their life.

Statement five stated that the belief that a colonist's children would be better or worse off would have been responded to by the colonists with a three for somewhat worse off. This was due to the anxiety level that was building as a result of the actions outlined in this two-year period.

There was no real way to utilize Section II of the instrument for this period so it was omitted. The average of the responses was 2.60 which would indicate that the colonists were somewhat complacent yet leaning toward dissatisfaction. This was considered fair since the period began with colonists feeling relatively at ease but beginning to shift toward dissatisfaction. The instrument should ideally measure the sentiment over the entire period so averaged out it would be somewhere near what the instrument suggested.

*Set 2:  1765-1766.*

This set began with the passage of the Stamp Act, another act of Parliament that served to irritate the colonists. The level of discontent continued to rise as evident in the rioting and looting that took place in major cities. The British government and the colonists appeared to be headed toward more violent confrontation.

The Stamp Act was passed on March 22, 1765 and was notable as the first direct tax on colonists. It was meant to help defray costs associated with the defense of the colonies and applied to printed documents, playing cards, and dice, among other items. It also asserted the jurisdictional right of the vice admiralty court, which did not use juries, in Nova Scotia to hear all cases related to the act. Schlesinger (1993) stated that its passage met "with universal colonial opposition" and raised the level of anxiety among the colonists by increasing "the likelihood that this tax will usher in others" and excited "fears of the erosion of the basic civil right of trial by jury" (p. 101).

A second act further added to the level of dissatisfaction among colonists. The Quartering Act was passed on March 24, 1765 and required colonists to provide shelter, food, and other items to British troops sent to America to defend it. This act was supported by the British military commander in America at the time, General Thomas Gage.

Reaction to the passage of these acts ranged from condemnation, organized responses, and riots to boycotts of English goods. James Otis stated that "one single act of Parliament had set people a-thinking in six months more than they had ever done in their whole lives before" (Lungguth, 1988, p. 54). Both the Virginia and Massachusetts legislatures passed resolutions that made statements against the actions of Parliament. Patrick Henry, a new member of the House of Burgesses, led the Virginia legislature by proposing seven resolutions that stated colonists had the same rights as British citizens and that taxes could only be imposed by chosen representatives, preferably colonial legislatures (Langguth, 1988, p. 69). It was during the debate where Henry made one of his famous statements: "if this be treason, make the most of it" (Schlesinger, 1993, p. 101). Massachusetts offered its own set of resolutions that asserted colonists possessed the same rights of British citizens that could not be taken away, there could be no property taken without consent, and that any attempt to do so were "infringements of our inherent and unalienable rights as men and British subjects" (House of Representatives of Massachusetts, 1765).

Other organized responses include the colonial Stamp Act Congress that passed resolutions requesting the repeal of the Stamp Act and the Sons of Liberty, a loosely formed group in various colonial towns that regularly employed violence as a means to get resignations of stamp agents and to prevent merchants from ordering imported goods (Schlesinger, 1993, pp. 101-102). The spring and summer of 1765 saw increased riots and looting in cities like Boston and New York City complete with the burning of effigies and warehouses (Langguth, 1988, pp. 56-59). Non-violent means were employed via

nonimportation acts put in place through the end of 1765 in all large colonial port cities

such as New York City, Boston, Philadelphia, and Charleston. Raphael (2002) added

that "by the end of 1765 the stamp distributors in all colonies except Georgia had

resigned their posts" (p. 15).

The acts of the colonies caused Parliament to reconsider the Stamp Act.

Benjamin Franklin and other colonists were called to England to present their grievances

to Parliament. Franklin was preferred because "he was a leading authority on the

American character, and he reminded his audience of the immense goodwill that

Americans had felt toward Britain only three years earlier" (Lungguth, 1988, p. 86).

Parliament, in March 1766, repealed the Stamp Act, which was greeted initially by

jubilation among colonists but was quickly followed by the Declaratory Act which stated

that Parliament had the right to pass any law that it chose to impose on the colonies.

The success of the riots against the Stamp Act emboldened New York tenant

farmers to revolt over land disputes with wealthy landowners. Rapheal (2002) suggested

that the "angry farmers, apparently powerless, stood tall in the face of their rulers, who

had to be bailed out by the British Army" and "contributed indirectly to the coming

Revolution by chipping away at the notion that a few men of prestige … could exploit

those beneath them with impunity" (p. 33). The two-year period ended with a mixed

level of uncertainty about future events.

*Set 2 Perceived Task Complexity.* The PTC was based on the relatively mixed

complexity that one could encounter in agriculture, trade, and business. The passage of

the Stamp Act and the anxiety that it brought on increased the uncertainty in many people's lives. An economic downturn that was made worse by The Stamp Act and The Currency Act and the loss of imported goods due to the nonimportation movement was difficult to bear. The colonists had to find ways to produce what they had formerly received from England and Ireland. This was not always easy due to the fact that resources were present but there were not many existing means to process or use them. There were some successes though as "Peter Hasenclever, a Prussian iron-monger establishes ironworks in New York and New Jersey" (Schlesinger, 1993, p. 100). The PTC score for this set was 2.67, which means that the environment was somewhat simple to slightly mixed.

*Set 2 Structural Leadership Profile.* George III was the leader again and he exerted the same level of leadership either directly or indirectly through Parliament, most of the colonial governors, and his new colonial military ruler General Thomas Gage. Due to these aspects the leadership score remained the same at 1.80 or very autocratic.

*Set 2 Structural Followership Profile.* Individuals like Sam Adams, Patrick Henry, Richard Lee, and Benjamin Franklin along with the Sons of Liberty were characteristic of the followers for this period. The riots, boycotts, and resolutions of colonial legislatures were actions of the followers that were utilized to complete the instrument. The followership score was 3.81, which means that the majority of followers of this period were most likely to be independent and in need of only minimal supervision. The congruence of the task environment, leadership, and followership styles was 1.34.

*Set 2 Social Satisfaction Instrument.* The fear of erosion of basic civil rights like a trial by jury, the actions of the British government, the riots, and looting created uncertainty and anxiety among many colonists. A major peace treaty with Chief Pontiac

and the repeal of The Stamp Act moderated some of the anxiety but the overall sentiment

was one of dissatisfaction. The Social Satisfaction Instrument score was 3.20.

*Set 3: 1767-1768.*

Parliament imposed new taxes, restricted colonial government even more than in

the past, and utilized the British military to police an increasingly restive public. The

colonists engaged in riots primarily over taxes, felt anxious over the increased presence

of the military, and bore more restrictions on self-rule.

British real estate taxes were reduced in 1767 and it was proposed that part of the

shortfall to the treasury be made up by increased taxes on the colonists. Chancellor of the

Exchequer Charles Townshend served "notice that he is designing a new revenue

instrument that will override the authority of the colonial legislative assemblies"

(Schlesinger, 1993, p. 104). The Townshend Acts pass Parliament in June of 1767 to

make up part of the shortfall and help cover the costs of defense for the colonies by

imposing import taxes on glass, paper, and tea, among other items needed and imported

by the colonists. Additional vice admiralty courts, that could try smugglers without a

jury, were established to assist in compliance. A further act of Parliament was to take

away the New York Assembly's powers for failing to adequately comply with the

Quartering Act.

The leader of this period, again, was George III but many other participants acted

on his behalf. Charles Townshend was influential but he died in September 1767.

Langguth (1988) suggested that George III established "a new impediment to

reconciliation with the colonies" by appointing his close friend "Lord North, who regretted the repeal of the Stamp Act and believed that the colonies were on the brink of

mutiny" (p. 99). Lord North once stated to Parliament that "America must fear you –

before she can love you" and he preferred to see "American prostrate at our feet"

(Langguth, 1988, p. 105). The Duke of Bedford was one who felt "that England [should]

punish the instigators of the Boston riots" by utilizing an old Henry VIII era law "that

would permit Parliament to bring men like James Otis and Samuel Adams to England,

where juries would convict them and judges would order them hanged" (Langguth, 1988,

p. 115). The general view among prominent governmental officials was one of an

immature group of spoiled subjects who just needed a little punishment.  It was felt "that

Americans could not endure the smell of gunpowder" (Langguth, 1988, p. 113).

Another of the King's antagonistic acts was to create the office of Secretary of

State for Colonial Affairs and appoint Lord Hillsborough to it.  It was Lord Hillsborough

who commanded all colonial governors to dissolve their respective assemblies if the

colonists continued in treasonous acts.  Some colonial governors such as Massachusetts

Governor Francis Bernard and, later, Thomas Hutchinson were instrumental in assisting

with the implementation of crown dictates.  Bernard fled from Boston after a series of

riots and public unrest stemming from new restrictions and his dissolution of the

Massachusetts general court caused him to fear for his life.  He was replaced by

Hutchinson, who was appointed and paid by the King.  Benjamin Franklin had this to say

about the colonial governors:

> generally [they were] strangers to the provinces they are sent to govern, have no
>
> estate, natural connection, or relation there to give them an affection for the
>
> country ... they come only to make money as fast as they can; are sometimes men

of vicious characters and broken fortunes, sent by a minister merely to get them

out of the way (Bailyn, 1992, p. 102).

John Dickinson, Samuel Adams, and John Hancock led the colonial protests over

the actions of the British government and their agents. John Dickinson, a Pennsylvania

farmer, attorney, and legislator wrote *Letters From a Farmer in Pennsylvania to the*

*Inhabitants of the British Colonies* that acknowledged Parliament's right to regulate trade

but stated that it had no right to raise revenue from colonial taxes and that as a result of

the suspension of the New York Assembly other colonies should worry (Schlesinger,

1993, p. 104). Sam Adams, on behalf of the Massachusetts House of Representatives of

which he was now a member, and with the help of James Otis, Thomas Cushing, and

Joseph Hawley quickly followed with a *Circular Letter to the Colonial Legislatures.*

Adams stated that taxes imposed for the "express purpose of raising a Revenue, are

Infringments [sic] of their natural & constitutional" and "that it will forever be

impracticable that they should be equally represented" in Parliament due to the distance

and expense of the undertaking (Massachusetts House of Representatives, 1768). Adams

became increasingly dissatisfied and had even suggested that citizens begin to arm

themselves for protection. He was also able to persuade the legislature "to pass a

resolution unanimously that no law – not merely no tax law – was binding on a colony

unless its own legislature passed it" (Langguth, 1988, p. 119).

John Hancock owned a ship named Liberty that sailed into Boston Harbor with a

cargo hold of wine that was not totally disclosed to customs officials and was thus

impounded. This act resulted in an angry mod that stormed through Boston and attacked

customs officials. Schlesinger (1993) stated that "the *Liberty* incident gained Hancock widespread popularity and instigated his entry into the political arena, under the tutelage of Samuel Adams" (p. 107). He would gradually become more involved in politics, both in Massachusetts and the other colonies as well. It was said that "John Hancock was New England's most popular man" (Langguth, 1988, p. 97).

Riots became more commonplace in the colonies during this period. Settlers in South Carolina complained about inadequate protection from an "Infernal Gang of Villains" while residents of North Carolina protested the oppression by corrupt leaders who "continually Squez'd [sic] and oppressed poor … families" for taxes, etc. (Raphael, 2002, p. 31). There were even riots by colonists in Norfolk, Virginia in 1768 against smallpox inoculations.

Nonimportation agreements against British goods began to be implemented in the colonies. Schlesinger (1993) added that merchants in New York agreed to cancel orders for all goods placed after August 15, 1768, to refuse imports after November 1, 1768 and to "do no business with merchants who do not support the provisions of the New York nonimportation agreement" (p. 107). The New York merchants, along with merchants in other colonies, vowed to keep the nonimportation agreements in place until Parliament repealed the Townshend Acts.

The nonimportation agreements led to efforts to increase the ability of the colonists to be self-sustaining. New England women played a large role in this effort. The Spinning Bees were women who traditionally made clothes for pastors but they began to do so for the community as a whole. Raphael (2002) stated that they "served both to advertise the making of cloth and to demonstrate that women could become patriots without departing from traditional concepts of femininity" (p. 136). Others chose

to find ways to manufacture the items that were previously acquired from England and
Ireland with colonial raw materials. Schlesinger (1993) stated that a New York City
committee was charged to "design a policy that will enhance New York industry and
lessen reliance on English imports of both necessities and luxury items" (p. 105). An
individual in Boston established its first foundry in an effort to cast type print for printing
presses used for newspapers and pamphlets that served a useful purpose in the years to
come.

Britain responded to increased hostility with military force. The frigate Romney
was sent to Boston at the request of customs officials. 4,000 British soldiers were sent to
Boston in the fall of 1768. This just infuriated New Englanders more with calls for
armed resistance. Bailyn (1992) said that one colonists asked "what can be worse to a
people who have tasted liberty" while others' "fear and hatred became edged with
contempt" (p. 114).

*Set 3 Perceived Task Complexity.* The task environment was influenced primarily
by the increased duties and the nonimportation agreements that followed. These initially
caused uncertainty as merchants and farmers looked to markets to sell their products and
get the items they needed to produce their goods. There were increased efforts to
establish more means to produce the things the colonies needed on their own as well as
selling more of their products that were previously sold to England to other colonists.
The PTC score for this period was 2.83.

*Set 3 Structural Leadership Profile.* George III continued to exert his influence
over the colonists either directly or through others. A new instrument was utilized

because George III exercised more control over the colonists but increasingly through others. The score ended up the same as the prior two periods at 1.80.

*Set 3 Structural Followership Profile.* The characteristics of followers were exhibited by the likes of Samuel Adams, John Hancock, John Dickinson, and others. Their actions and the actions of those that they influenced were duplicated in other areas of the colonies. The score from this period's instrument was 3.81. The degree of congruency was 1.34.

*Set 3 Social Satisfaction Instrument.* The degree of social satisfaction was influenced in this period by anxiety produced by the actions of Parliament and their agents and the increased presence of the British military in the colonies. Langguth (1988) added that "the soldiers disrupted [Boston's] daily routine by parading through the streets and disturbed church services on Sunday by changing the guard" (p. 120). The score for this period was 3.40.

*Set 4: 1769-1770.*

The events of this period were a continued escalation of the tension between the British government and the colonists. The leader remained the same, the followers were represented by the same and some new individuals, and the environment continued to evolve as a result of the actions of both sides.

Nonimportation agreements were implemented in the colonies throughout 1769 in protest of the Townshend Acts. Some focused on banning imported English goods, others such as Virginia banned English imports as well as slaves, while others banned the imports but also goods from other colonies that did not support the nonimportation agreements (Schlesinger, 1993, pp. 108 – 109). Sam Adams wrote an article that was published in the Boston Gazette in February 1769 that tried to rationalize a stronger approach than nonimportation agreements. He felt that in the past, doctrines of *"passive obedience, non-resistance,* the *divine hereditary right* of kings" were the norm but that progress in "human affairs" now meant that oppression of citizens by their government against the "three great and primary rights of *personal security, personal liberty* and *private property"* entitled them to use force if necessary to restore their rights (Adams, 1769). George Washington, an upcoming influential Virginian, presented Virginia's version of nonimportation developed by George Mason, a friend of Washington's. Washington made clear to Mason in a letter to him that he felt "no man shou'd [*sic*] scruple, or hesitate a moment to use [arms] in defence [*sic*] of so valuable a blessing" yet it "should be the last resource" (Washington, 1997, p. 130).

The role of women continued to be significant in boycotting goods. They signed "petitions which competed favorably with the most flamboyant of male polemics" as they promised to abstain from tea in order to 'save this abused Country from Ruin and Slavery'" (Raphael, 2002, pp. 140 -141).

King George III was still firmly in control of the British actions through such agents as Parliament (to an extent), the English Board of Trade, Lord North, and appointed governors like Hutchinson of Massachusetts and Botetourt of Virginia. The English Board of Trade considered revoking the Townshend Acts as the colonists' nonimportation agreements began to seriously affect British Merchants. Lord North became Prime Minister on January 31, 1770 and it was known that, although he may have been willing to repeal some of the Townshend Acts, he was against total repeal because it "might indicate weakness on the part of the British government" (Schlesinger,

1993, p. 109). Hutchinson continued to be governor of Massachusetts and was more or less the puppet of the crown as he was aware he could be removed at any time.

Skirmishes turned violent in 1770, first in New York and, then more tragically, in Boston. The Sons of Liberty, headed by Alexander McDougall, fought with a platoon of British soldiers on Golden Hill in New York resulting in some wounded but no deaths. This was followed a few weeks later by the Boston Massacre in which British soldiers opened fire on a rowdy mob. The result was that anyone who doubted that the role of a standing army was to "terrify a populace into compliance with tyrannical wills were silenced by that event" (Bailyn, 1992, p. 116). Nine British soldiers were arrested by civil authorities and put on trial for murder. A noted clergyman and Tory, Mather Byles, responded to the violence by asking whether it was better "to be ruled by one tyrant three thousand miles away or by three thousand tyrants not one mile away" (Langguth, 1988, p. 154).

John Adams had the task of defending the soldiers and at one point called the Boston mob "a motley rabble of saucy boys, Negroes and mulattoes, Irish teagues and outlandish jacktars" while the soldiers, "wretched conservators of the peace," were placed in the awkward position where their deployment "in a populous town will always occasion two mobs where they prevent one" (McCullough, 2001, p. 67). Seven of the nine soldiers were acquitted and the other two, found guilty of manslaughter, were branded as punishment.

The actions of the colonists and pressure from British merchants finally led the crown to rescind the Townshend Acts, with the exception of a small tax that remained on tea, while the Quartering Act was allowed to expire without a renewal. One by one the colonies revoked their nonimportation agreement as an uneasy calm returned.

The colonies continued in their efforts to become self-sufficient. Dartmouth College was founded as the ninth college in America, a glassmaking factory began producing glass in Pennsylvania, and regular monthly mail service between the southern and northern colonies were linked by a transfer point in Suffolk, Virginia (Schlesinger, 1993, pp. 108 – 109). The population in 1770 was estimated to be 2.2 million people.

*Set 4 Perceived Task Complexity.* The environment of this period was one of increased uncertainty and anxiety in the beginning that shifted to a tentative calm toward the end of the period. There were continued attempts to improve their self-sufficiency through educational opportunities, industrial development, and communication systems. Their ability to acquire needed resources, technical knowledge, and capital was still limited. The PTC score for this period was 2.92.

*Set 4 Structural Leadership Profile.* The influence of George III as a leader was strongly felt as he either exercised power directly or, more frequently, through cabinet offices like the English Board of Trade, close associates like Lord North, and the colonial governors. The score continued to be the same as the prior three periods at 1.80.

*Set 4 Structural Followership Profile.* The characteristics of followers were affected by the events of the period and represented by individuals like Sam Adams, John Adams, and George Washington. Their sentiments were shared by many in the north and the south. The score from this period's instrument was 3.75. The degree of congruency was 1.30.

*Set 4 Social Satisfaction Instrument.* The anxiety of taxes and uncertainty of how many rights would be suspended or taken away after violent actions on both sides were moderated by the restoration of an uneasy calm at the end of the period. The score for this period was 2.80.

*Set 5: 1771-1772.*

The beginning of this set was a continuation of the uneasy calm that was in place at the end of 1770. The calm ended as both sides began to ratchet up their efforts to get the other side to give in to their respective demands.

North Carolina, one of the more moderate colonies, began 1771 by enacting the Bloody Act, which equated rioting with treason. The act was inspired by the rebellions of settlers in the western part of the colony. The settlers were upset over the unequal representation in the colonial assembly and perceived "charges of extortion and oppression against the politically powerful eastern part of the colory" (Schlesinger, 1993, p. 110). The movement resulted in an armed expedition led by the colonial governor to successfully suppress the rebellion. The end of the rebellion came at a time when the last nonimportation agreement was dropped in Virginia.

Violence returned to the northern colonies as a British customs schooner, the Gaspee, was raided and burned off the Rhode Island coast after it ran aground. This was a serious escalation of the feud between Britain and the colonies because a royal ship had been destroyed. Governor Hutchinson called for the execution of those responsible as the only way to minimize the risk of future attacks (Langguth, 1988, p. 169). King George III announced a 500 pound reward for the capture of those involved and that all would be sent to England for trial, a constant fear of colonists.

The counsel of Sam Adams was sought by New Englanders in order to determine what they should do in the face of an impending increase of British forces in the colonies. He turned the Gaspee event around, implied that the colonists were provoked by Britain, and suggested that all "colonists must realize that an attack on one province was an attack on them all" (Langguth, 1988, p. 169). Adams then wrote and distributed a pamphlet all over the colony that was, among other things, critical of Hutchinson's attachment to the crown. Bailyn (1992) stated that it contained "a list of twelve items, which took seventeen pamphlet pages to describe" violations of the rights of the colonists and Massachusetts in particular (p. 117). It was signed by 260 different towns in Massachusetts.

Benjamin Franklin began work on his autobiography, in which he attributed his success and happiness to God's "divine providence" and the constant efforts at self-improvement (Franklin, 1994, pp. 2 – 17). His actions became more prominent during this time frame as he was an agent in London for Massachusetts. Franklin, "angered when the Ministry in London sent troops to Boston" was able to obtain copies of letters from Governor Hutchinson to a member of the government in London and mail them to the speaker of the Massachusetts House (Langguth, 1988, p. 171). The letters, which were not supposed to be released to the public, were circulated and soon to be read aloud throughout the colony by people like John Adams. Hutchinson's image already suffered from his move to punish Boston for the Tea Party by moving the legislature to Cambridge to make it more difficult for assemblymen to do colonial business. The letters provided fuel for the fire as Sam Adams "had been suggesting that Hutchinson was engaged in a secret correspondence aimed at destroying America s liberties" (Langguth, 1988, p. 172).

John Adams, "who took no cheer from his election" to the Massachusetts House, was another rising influence among the colonists (Langguth, 1988, p. 164). He continued his transformation from practicing law toward more involvement in civic affairs as he gained favor with Bostonians and others in the colony and elsewhere. His view on government was that it was "nothing more than the combined force of society" along equal lines and that the "preservation of liberty depends upon the intellectual and moral character of the people" (McCullough, 2001, pp. 69 – 70). The role he played was on of conservatism among the more radical individuals like his cousin Sam. The events around him though continued to shape his actions and move him away from his conservatism toward more moderate ones.

The environment was further strained as a banking crisis emerged in the British financial system in July of 1772. The result was a "widespread reduction of credit" that caused colonial merchants to liquidate inventories and caused severe strain that would last until 1776 (Schlesinger, 1993, p. 111). This dealt a blow to the colonies as they tried to develop some level of self-sufficiency.

*Set 5 Perceived Task Complexity.* The environment of this period was one of increased attempts by the colonists to improve their self-sufficiency. The steady progress toward that goal was severely hampered by the inability to obtain capital as a result of the banking crisis. The PTC score for this period was 2.83.

*Set 5 Structural Leadership Profile.* The influence of George III continued to be felt through the actions of Parliament and colonial governors. The score slipped somewhat to 1.75 as the British were determined to bring about compliance with more force if necessary.

*Set 5 Structural Followership Profile.* The characteristics of followers were represented by individuals like Sam Adams, John Adams, and Benjamin Franklin. They represented radicalism, conservatism, and moderation respectively. The score from this period's instrument was 3.75. The degree of congruency was 1.33.

*Set 5 Social Satisfaction Instrument.* The rebellion in North Carolina, the burning of the Gaspee, and the banking crises continued to fuel the uncertainty that colonists felt. The score for this period was 2.80.

*Set 6: 1773-1774.*

The British Parliament continued in its efforts to restore some order to the colonies while the colonists took more steps to resist. The end of this two year period was a realization for many that the problems between the two parties were not going to end peaceably.

Parliament passed legislation in the spring of 1773 that removed all but one of the taxes on imported tea. The Tea Act gave the East India Company the right to sell tea directly to agents that put the company "in a position to undersell the law-abiding colonial merchants who have to purchase English tea through the agency of middlemen at higher prices" (Schlesinger, 1993, p. 112). This was a slap in the face of many colonists and eliminated any goodwill that may have existed as a result of the removal of most tea taxes. Langguth (1988) added that "this time, Bostonians were alarmed, even without prompting from Samuel Adams, that the new method for selling tea could be applied to other commodities …. [and] then all trade would disappear" and reduce Americans to "fur trappers and lumberjack" (p. 174). The reactions in many cities included the demand

for resignations in Philadelphia and Boston and the firing of broadsides in New York City

to warn "any harbor pilots not to guide any vessels bearing tea into the harbor"

(Schlesinger, 1993, p. 112). It was at this point that the stage was set for one of the most

memorable events in American history.

The Dartmouth was the first of three ships carrying tea to enter the Boston harbor

in late November 1773. A meeting was held in New York by the Sons of Liberty to

condemn tea consignees as enemies while a meeting in Boston was convened to decide

what to do about the Dartmouth. They decide to send the ship back to England with the

tea but Governor Hutchinson orders the ships not to leave until the tax was paid. It was

then decided by a group led by Samuel Adams that they were not going to pay the tax nor

send the ship back. Langguth (1988) stated that "Adams rose from his chair and said

'This meeting can do nothing more to save the country,'" which was the signal to head

for the ship while John Hancock added "Let every man do what is right in his own eyes"

(p. 179). The group then proceeded to the ship dressed as Mohawks and dumped the tea

into the harbor. The tea ship London in Charleston harbor was seized two days later by

customs officials for nonpayment of the tax in South Carolina. An event similar to the

dumping of tea in Boston followed in New York City a few months later when the Sons

of Liberty dressed as Indians and dumped tea into the New York harbor.

These acts were just one of the protests by colonists that escalated the tension.

Women again played a role when they were told that "if they refrained from drinking tea,

they could convince the British 'that American patriotism extends even to the Fair Sex'"

(Raphael, 2002, p. 138).

The Hutchinson letters were published in June 1773 despite the pledge by the Massachusetts assembly to keep them private. Langguth (1988) stated that the even the colonists outside of Massachusetts were outraged as "Hutchinson was burned in effigy as far away as Philadelphia" (p. 172). The colonists petitioned King George III for the removal of Hutchinson but after a review it was decided by the English Privy Council not to do so. Benjamin Franklin was removed from as Deputy Postmaster General for America as a result of the Hutchinson letters. Finally, Hutchinson's career as Massachusetts Governor came to an end when General Gage landed in Boston with more troops to relieve him of his office.

Parliament then responded with a series of legislation known collectively as the Coercive Acts that Bailyn (1992) said "no liberty-loving people could tolerate" (p. 118). Lord North introduced the first act, The Boston Port Act, as a response to the Boston Tea Party. This act banned all ships not carrying fuel or supplies from entering Boston's harbor as North stated "obedience, not indemnification, will be the test of the Bostonians" (Langguth, 1988, p. 189). The effect on Boston, a major trading center in the colonies, was devastating. McCullough (2001) added that "shut off fro the sea, Boston was doomed" (p. 70). The second of the acts was the Administration of Justice Act which protected British officials from trials in the colonies since they would now have to take place in England and only under limited circumstances. Another, The Massachusetts Government Act, "stripped from the people of Massachusetts the protection of the British constitution by giving over all the 'democratic' elements of the province's government" to appointees of the King and other British officials (Bailyn, 1992, p. 119).

Two additional acts, The Quebec Act and an amended and revised Quartering Act, were also passed thus imposing additional restraints on the colonists. The Quebec Act was primarily focused on government of Canada and religious tolerance but it was the last part that infuriated the colonists. The boundary of Canada was extended southward into westward territories claimed by Virginia, Connecticut, and Massachusetts. The amended Quartering Act applied to all colonies and allowed troops to seize all unoccupied buildings. Thomas Jefferson responded by stating in 1774 that:

single acts of tyranny may be ascribed to the accidental opinion of the day … a series of oppressions, begun at a distinguished period and pursued unalterably through every change of ministers, too plainly prove a deliberate and systematical plan of reducing us to slavery (Bailyn, 1992, pp. 119 – 120).

When the Virginia House of Burgesses was dissolved in 1774 by Governor Dunmore it was proposed by the members that a congress of all colonies be convened. All colonies, with the exception of Georgia, agreed by the end of summer to send delegates to it. The First Continental Congress was opened on September 5, 1774 and during the course of it the Suffolk Resolves were passed that stated the Coercive Acts were "unconstitutional and hence not to be obeyed," colonial tax bodies should be established to hold taxes in escrow, local militias should be established and armed, and that economic sanctions should be applied to England (Schlesinger, 1993, pp. 114 – 115). Additional resolutions were aimed at addressing all grievances the colonists had as well as asserting their rights once more. George Washington, in a letter to Bryan Fairfax, summed up a common view of Virginians that the time had arrived "when we must assert our Rights, or Submit to every Imposition that can be heap'd [sic] upon us; till custom and use, will make us tame, & abject Slaves, as the Blacks we Rule over with such arbitrary Sway" (Washington, 1997, p. 158). The Congress adjourned in late fall with the intention of holding a second one in 1775.

Armed conflict continued to escalate as General Gage seized the Massachusetts colonial arsenal at Charlestown in September 1774 and Massachusetts militia attacked an arsenal in Portsmouth, New Hampshire. The Massachusetts House was dissolved by General Gage and elections canceled, which prompted the members to convene a Provincial Congress in Salem. Schlesinger (1988) added that "with Hancock as president, the delegates launched the colony's first government independent of the British king," retained the tax revenue collected to date, and established a Committee of Safety to manage the new militia known as the Minute Men (p. 217). The actions of the Massachusetts delegates came to be known as the Massachusetts Revolution of 1774. British troops withdrew back to Boston for the winter as "General Gage reported back to London: 'the Flames of Sedition' had 'spread universally throughout the Country beyond Conception'" (Raphael, 2002, p. 57). It was also at this time that loyalists began to leave the colonies for England due to concerns of an impending conflict.

*Set 6 Perceived Task Complexity.* The degradation in the environment was related to the increased uncertainty of the future and the real possibility that any imports above bare necessities would be difficult to acquire. The exodus of loyalists who were likely to possess more resources than the average colonist was a severe drain. The result was that many of the primary economic factors required for economic development were in short supply. The PTC score for this period was 2.50.

*Set 6 Structural Leadership Profile.* The severity of response from the British government as it tried to reign in the colonists resulted in more restrictions on liberty and property. King George III, Thomas Hutchinson, Lord North, and General Gage were significant forces as force was exerted. The score continued to slip to 1.65 as the leadership style of George III and his agents shifted more toward autocratic behavior.

*Set 6 Structural Followership Profile.* The colonists began to realize that they would be better of governing themselves. This was most likely due to the events of the past ten years and the majority's changing views on self-government. The score from this period's instrument was 3.94. The degree of congruency was 1.53.

*Set 6 Social Satisfaction Instrument.* The Coercive Acts, the rebellions, and the emigration of loyalists were signs of dissatisfaction. The period ended with the revolution in Massachusetts. The score for this period was 3.20.

*Set 7: 1775-1776.*

This period marked the last time that the colonists considered themselves to be subjects of the crown. Independence was declared and a new group of individuals emerged to lead the new confederation in its efforts to find a government more akin to their beliefs and desires.

The petitions from the First Continental Congress were delivered to Parliament in the early part of 1775. They were subsequently dismissed by the members who were not interested in conciliation. The colonies had some supporters like Lord Chatham and Edmund Burke in Parliament. Lord Chatham was more interested in trying to find a workable solution to the impasse by requesting that Parliament remove some of the British troops, recognize the Continental Congress, and allow the colonists to have some say in taxation. This request was also dismissed by Parliament, who went further in February of 1775 by declaring Massachusetts, in which delegates had met earlier that month to prepare for the defense of the colony, to be in a state of rebellion. More troops landed in Massachusetts in late February and tried to seize an arsenal in Salem but were repulsed. King George III followed with the New England Restraining Act, which closed all trade among all New England colonies with any country but Britain and banned North Atlantic fishing by mid-summer. The act also stated that the other colonies would be added if they joined the nonimportation agreements put forth at the First Continental Congress. The nonimportation agreements were in effect by all 13 colonies by April of 1775.

General Gage received an order from Parliament on April 14, 1775 to "use all necessary force to implement the Coercive and other acts, and to strike preemptively to circumvent further buildup of the colonial military machine" (Schlesinger, 1993, p. 117). He then ordered a contingent of troops to march toward Concord to destroy an armory there. The British were met at Lexington where a group of Minute Men confronted them. The troops then pushed on to Concord where they were again met by Massachusetts militia, who subsequently harassed the British all the way back to Boston, with 49 Americans and 73 British killed. Four days later the Massachusetts Provincial Congress began the call-up of its militia and sent out a request for assistance from all other colonies.

The Second Continental Congress was called to order on May 10, 1775 with the election of Peyton Randolph as President followed by the election of John Hancock as President on May 24, 1775. The delegates passed a series of resolutions aimed at preparing for colonial defense by establishing a Continental Army with George

Washington as the supreme commander and a $2,000,000 issue of securities to raise

money for its support. The first declaration of independence came from Mecklenburg,

North Carolina when the residents decided to "annul all British implemented and derived

laws, suspend the royal government of the colony by placing all power in hands of the

provincial congress, and brand those accepting royal commissions as traitors"

(Schlesinger, 1993, p. 118).

Despite these actions there was an attempt at peace and reconciliation with the

Olive Branch Petition adopted by Congress and sent to King George III. The King

refused to even look at it and subsequently declared that all colonies were in a state of

rebellion. He followed later in the year with a proclamation that closed all trade with the

colonies. Congress responded by declaring that all trade was open except with Britain

and its possessions.

Not all colonists were for the move toward independence. Loyalist movements

were in place in all colonies to some degree. Battles took place in Virginia and North

Carolina in late 1775 and early 1776 between loyalists and independence-minded militia

in which the loyalists were defeated.

Thomas Paine was a major influence on the thoughts of Americans at this point in

time with the publication of *Common Sense* in early 1776. He echoed themes proposed

by Locke, Hobbes, and others that government is a necessary evil, "in its worst state an

intolerable one," in which one gives "up a part of his property to furnish means for the

protection of the rest" (Paine, 1997, p. 3). His assertions were based on variations of the

natural law and state of nature arguments put forth by earlier European philosophers that man was self-interested, organized into societies for protection from each other, and that some rights had to be given up in exchange for protection. Paine (1997) added "here then is the origin and rise of government; namely, a mode rendered necessary by the inability of moral virtue to govern the world; here too is the design and end of government, viz. freedom and security" (p. 5). The fight for independence was vital and success would come with the unity of all. He argued further that monarchies were evil because they possessed more power than necessary and that the virtue that one monarch may possess is not hereditary and is oppressive on a country's posterity. His final recommendation was a form of government with a large and equal number of representatives because "a small number of electors, or a small number of representatives, are equally dangerous" (Paine, 1997, p. 42). John Adams agreed with this assertion by stating that "all good government was republican" and that its assembly should be "an exact portrait in miniature of the people at large" (McCullough, 2001, p. 102). Jefferson, who read Common Sense, also believed in the elimination of aristocracy as well because he felt it was "essential to a well ordered republic" (Cunningham, 1987, p. 56).

The independence movement gained steam in the spring of 1776 as North Carolina became the first colony to instruct its delegates to press for independence. The view toward a loose confederation of colonies was put forth when Congress passed a resolution that authorized the formation of 13 provincial governments. The formal resolution for independence in Congress was put forth by Virginian Richard Henry Lee. Lee stated:

> that these United Colonies are, and of right ought to be, free and independent
>
> States, that they are absolved from all allegiance to the British Crown, and that all

political connection between them and the State of Great Britain is, and ought to

be, totally dissolved (Langguth, 1988, p. 343).

Congress then ordered John Adams, Ben Franklin, Thomas Jefferson, and others to come

up with a declaration of independence, the draft of which was delegated to Thomas

Jefferson. The design of a continental confederation structure was also delegated to a

committee headed by John Dickinson. Washington (1997) felt that the design was

important because "if the foundation is badly laid the superstructure must be bad" (p.

224). New York's delegation, under orders to abstain from voting, was the only one not

to vote for approval of the Declaration of Independence on July 2, 1776. The New York

delegates voted on July 9, 1776 to support the Declaration of Independence. The

confederation agreement for the colonies was presented to Congress on July 12, 1776.

An attempt by the British at resolving the independence movement was attempted

by Lord Howe at Staten Island on September 11, 1776. He met with John Adams, Ben

Franklin, and Edmund Rutledge to discuss peace but one of his conditions was that the

colonists revoke the Declaration of Independence. The meeting ended and conflict

continued through the end of the year, culminating in the surprise and needed attack by

Washington on the Hessians at Trenton in December, which provided hope for an

uncertain nation-to-be.

Other notable events of the time period included the establishment of a post office

with Ben Franklin as the head and the first abolition society, which was founded by

Franklin and Dr. Benjamin Rush. The American economy at this time was summed up

by Bryant and Dethloff (1990) as "a fairly complex system of agencies, partnerships,

correspondents, creditors, and instruments of trade" and that the "unusually rapid expansion of American business threatened the authority and 'liberty' of the English merchant" (p. 53). The continued efforts at self-sufficiency combined with an entrepreneurial spirit were major driving forces behind the changing economic environment.

*Set 7 Perceived Task Complexity.* The external environment that the colonies experienced continued the move away from a simplistic society dependent on the colonial master toward a self-sufficient one. The colonists realized as a result of trade restrictions and voluntary nonimportation agreements that they could produce the items they wanted and needed. The PTC score for this period was 3.08.

*Set 7 Structural Leadership Profile.* There were two leaders for this period. King George III was the leader for 5 of the 24 months. John Hancock became the leader of the colonies in May of 1775 when he was elected as president of the Continental Congress.

Table 3 - Calculation of weights for set 7 multiple influential leaders

| Leader number, n | Leader name | Influence time, m (in months / 24) | Time factor, t (m/24*0.5) | Magnitude / Scope, s (from little - 1 - to great - 3) | Mag. / scope factor, f (s/3*0.5) | Sum of factors, x (t+f) | Weight, w (x / sum of x's) |
|---|---|---|---|---|---|---|---|
| 1 | King George II | 5 | 0.1041667 | 2 | 0.33333333 | 0.4375 | 0.375 |
| 2 | John Hancock | 19 | 0.3958333 | 2 | 0.33333333 | 0.729167 | 0.625 |
| | | | | | Sum: | 1.166667 | 1 |

Two leadership profiles were used for this period utilizing the weights calculated from Table 3. George III's score was the same at 1.65 while John Hancock's was 3.45. The weighted leadership score was 2.78 (1.65 for George III times 0.375 added to 3.45 for John Hancock times 0.675).

*Set 7 Structural Followership Profile.* Followers such as John Adams, Thomas Paine, Thomas Jefferson, Benjamin Franklin, and George Washington had views that were characteristic of the rest of the Americans at this time. The score from this period's instrument was 3.62. The views slipped somewhat from the last period as new leadership was in place that was more responsive to the needs of the followers. The degree of congruency was 0.56.

*Set 7 Social Satisfaction Instrument.* Dissatisfaction in this period was high right up to the beginning of armed hostility and the Declaration of Independence. Some sense of satisfaction was restored as the colonies declared their independence, set up a government more conducive to their beliefs, and then began a defensive campaign to keep what they had established.

A change from using just section I of the Social Satisfaction Instrument was done in this set to reflect the composition of the Continental Congress. This was an added measure of satisfaction as the members of each colony's assembly nominated delegates to Congress based on a variety of factors, one of which probably had something to do with how well nominated individuals were representing the views of each colony. Since there was only one branch of the Congress only subsection 1 of Section II was used. Turnover in the Continental Congress was 44%. The score for this period was 1.88.

*Set 8: 1777-1778.*

This period was one that saw increased battles between American and British forces and the establishment of a new form of government for the colonies. It was also a time when former followers became leaders and despite opportunities for peace the colonists decided to pursue full independence.

The period began with some jubilation over Washington's victory over the Hessians in Trenton and, soon after, Princeton before he settled into winter quarters in Morristown, New Jersey. It was at this time that residents of the western part of New Hampshire declared independence in an area claimed by both New Hampshire and New York. The name of the new entity was the Republic of New Connecticut. Six months later it was renamed Vermont and was significant in that its constitution specifically called for suffrage for all men and banned slavery.

The committee charged with designing a plan of confederation presented Congress with the Articles of Confederation. The plan was endorsed and sent to the colonies for ratification.

Military events dominated 1777 as massacres in the western frontier by Indians allied with Britain caused "colonists to enlist for military service in ever-increasing numbers" (Schlesinger, 1993, p. 125). General Washington and the Continental Army had made many mistakes in the early parts of the war and so victories were important for morale. Ellis (2002) stated that Washington soon came to realize that just as victories were important if the Continental Army "remained intact as a fighting force, the American Revolution remained alive" (p. 130).

The task of holding his army together was difficult for Washington. Raphael (2002) pondered that, while a new set of clothing was offered to new recruits, it was uncertain how long it would last (p. 111). The lack of adequate supplies was not the only problem as a plot to replace Washington as commanding general threatened to disrupt his efforts. The plot was known as the Conway Cabal after Major Thomas Conway. Washington (1997) stated in a letter to Virginia delegate Richard Henry Lee that his goals were strictly focused on serving his country and that he had been through "more than most Men are aware of, to harmonize so many discordant parts; but it will be impossible for me to be of any further service, if such insufferable difficulties are thrown in my way" (p. 276). Conway resigned and Washington continued as commander.

The Battle of Saratoga was another defining military victory for the Americans because a major British force surrendered. This surrender not only was a positive sign for the war-weary Americans but it would be a significant reason that France decided to officially recognize America's independence. The recognition was followed by treaties of alliance and commerce between France and America. The colonists gained a market for their goods and a place to obtain items that could not be produced in sufficient numbers.

The British felt compelled to offer the colonists another chance at conciliation after they became aware of the treaties between America and France. A British Peace Commission with "wide powers to negotiate with the American revolutionaries" was sent to Philadelphia in June of 1778 to negotiate (Schlesinger, 1993, p. 128). Congress was also aware of the implications of the treaties with France and thus rejected the peace offers as independence, rather than conciliation, became their goal. Not long after Congress rejected the peace offering France declared war on England. Washington (1997) was reluctantly happy that some relief was forthcoming but cautioned that it was "a maxim founded on the universal experience of mankind, that no nation is to be trusted farther than it is bound by its interest" (p. 329).

John Hancock was President of Congress until November of 1777 and was followed by Henry Laurens. Laurens was from South Carolina and served until mid-

December 1778. Not much information was available on his beliefs but under his watch

Congress continued to focus on funding the war, lobbied for the passage of the Articles of

Confederation, signed treaties with France, rejected peace offerings from the British, and

nominated Benjamin Franklin to be America's representative to France in late 1778.

There was some discontent with the ability of Congress to perform necessary functions as

Washington (1997), in a letter to Virginia delegate Benjamin Harrison, that:

> The Public believes ... that the States at this time are badly represented, and that
>
> the great, and important concerns of the nation are horribly conducted, for want
>
> either of abilities or application in the Members, or through discord and party
>
> views of some individuals; that they should be so, is to be lamented more at this
>
> time, than formerly, as we are far advanced in the dispute (p. 332).

Thomas Jefferson's views continued to be influential in Congress as well even

though he had returned to Virginia as a delegate to the Virginia House of Delegates. One

matter that he weighed in on as important to republican principles of government was the

education of the populace. Jefferson, known as a "veritable legislative drafting bureau,"

introduced a bill in December 1778 and again in 1780 in which "he extolled the vital

importance of education to republican government" (Cunningham, 1987, pp. 57-59).

Women continued to be force to reckon with in terms of fighting the war. They

were considered as patriotic as the men and instrumental as resources to supply items

needed that were in short supply. Washington's view on women was summed up by

Raphael (2002) as gratuitous and that they deserved "an equal place with any who have

preceded them in the walk of female patriotism" (p. 146).

The patriotic view was not shared by all as loyalists struggled to survive in environments that were, at times, quite hostile. Raphael (2002) suggested that loyalists were those "who professed a continuing allegiance" to King George III, those "who passively accepted the legitimate authority of the British government," and those "who contributed to the loyalist cause for self-serving reasons without cherishing any special feelings" for Britain or its government (p. 184). The presence of loyalists was strongest in the south and weakest in the north. Some loyalists joined with the British and Indians in armed conflict against the independence-minded forces, especially in New York and Pennsylvania. Congress weighed in with their opinion of the loyalists in 1777 that required the confiscation of their property to help pay for the war (Schlesinger, 1993, p. 100).

*Set 8 Perceived Task Complexity.* The colonies were shut out from the external world by the end of the last set but that began to change with the signing of the commerce treaty with France. The colonies continued to raise funds from overseas governments hostile to England. The efforts of industrial-minded colonists were able to provide some of the items that a young nation needed to fight a war and sustain it in domestic areas. The score for this period was 3.08.

*Set 8 Structural Leadership Profile.* John Hancock served as President of the Continental Congress for 10 months. Henry Laurens was elected and served until December 1778. Not much is known about his personal profile so the actions of Congress under his watch were considered to be fairly consistent with his and, as such, were used to fill out the instrument. The calculation of leader weights can be found in Table 4.

Table 4 - Calculation of weights for set 8 multiple influential leaders

| Leader number, n | Leader name | Influence time, m (in months / 24) | Time factor, t (m/24*0.5) | Magnitude / Scope, s (from little - 1 - to great - 3) | Mag. / scope factor, f (s/3*0.5) | Sum of factors, x (t+f) | Weight, w (x / sum of x's) |
|---|---|---|---|---|---|---|---|
| 1 | John Hancock | 10 | 0.2083333 | 2 | 0.33333333 | 0.541667 | 0.541667 |
| 2 | Henry Laurens | 14 | 0.2916667 | 1 | 0.16666667 | 0.458333 | 0.458333 |
| | | | | | Sum: | 1 | 1 |

John Hancock's instrument score was the same from set 7 at 3.45 while Laurens and Congress received a 3.85. The two scores were calculated using the weighted values to give a score for this period of 3.63.

*Set 8 Structural Followership Profile.* The followers of this period included soldiers, women, and, to a lesser extent, the loyalists. Other notable followers were George Washington, Thomas Jefferson, and Benjamin Franklin. Their views were summarized and resulted in a score for the set of 3.31. The congruence was 0.36.

*Set 8 Social Satisfaction Instrument.* The satisfaction prevalent in this set ranged from uncertainty that resulted from military losses to elation when victories occurred. There was also continued anxiety among western settlers as loyalists combined with British soldiers and Indians to raid settlements. A growing dissatisfaction was present with some of the weaknesses of Congress in terms of providing for the needs of soldiers and citizens. Turnover in the Continental Congress was 62.4%. The score for this period was 2.25.

*Set 9: 1779-1780.*

The leaders and followers of this period strived to deal with the wartime environment as it entered its fourth year. The strain of battlefield losses and an economy that could not provide for the needs of the Americans pushed the nation to the brink of disaster.

The ratio of battlefield victories and losses favored the British throughout this period. The fighting raged in all of the colonies with all of the colonial militias, the Continental Army, and France on one side and loyalists, Britain, and their Indian allies on the other side. Spain joined the war against Britain in June of 1779 in order to attempt to gain Gibraltar and Florida from the British. The additional pressure on Britain was welcomed but was not enough to turn the tide of war. Washington (1997) stated that by end of 1779 "the combined fleets of France and Spain last year were greatly superior of those of the enemy: The enemy nevertheless sustained no material damage, and at the close of the campaign have given a very important blow to our allies" (p. 374). The Americans were able to win enough battles to stay alive but not much more than that.

Congress elected John Jay as President toward the end of 1778. Schlesinger (1993) described Jay as one who possessed "sound judgment, moral rectitude, sense of duty toward his country, and responsible attitude toward his work" (p. 130). John Jay was a New Yorker who practiced law prior to his appointment as a delegate to the First and Second Continental Congress. He originally "represented the conservative interests of colonial merchants who feared independence because it could result in mob rule by the democratic majority" but changed his mind after the Declaration of Independence and put his full support behind the movement (Schlesinger, 1993, p. 130). He was President until his appointment in September of 1779 as minister to Spain, where he tried unsuccessfully to get a signed alliance and funds for the war. Samuel Huntington of Connecticut, of whom not much information is known, was elected to replace Jay

Washington struggled to keep the Continental Army together throughout the next two years. He and his troops entered winter quarters in Morristown, New Jersey where they faced "a worse winter than the previous one" as they encountered "low morale, low supplies, desertions and attempts at mutiny" (Schlesinger, 1993, p. 132). The situation grew worse in March 1780 as Congress passed the Forty To One Act that changed the redemption value of the Continental currency to one-fortieth of its original value, essentially making it worthless. Washington (1997) wrote to New York delegate Governour Morris and suggested that:

> The rapid decay or our currency, the extinction of public spirit, the
>
> increasing rapacity of the times, the want of harmony in our councils, the
>
> declining zeal of the people, the discontents, and distresses of the officers
>
> of the army; and may I add, the prevailing security and insensibility to
>
> danger, are symptoms, in my eye of a most alarming nature (p. 349).

Connecticut soldiers attempted a revolt in the winter camp as they demanded rations and payment of back pay. Pennsylvania troops restored order and two men were executed. Washington sent a letter three days later to Virginia delegate Joseph Reed to express his concern with the lack of attention given to the army. He stated that "the country is in such a state of insensibility and indifference to its interests, that I dare not flatter myself with any change for the better" (Washington, 1997, p. 373). A common problem was that each colony chose to fulfill their wartime quota of supplies as each desired because Congress was essentially powerless to enforce them. General Washington felt compelled to send circular letters in August and October 1780 to all of the states to beg for supplies for the army that was defending each one's interests. The final blow to Washington for this period was the treason of Benedict Arnold, who was a close associate of the general.

Congress was able to get the colonies of New York and Connecticut to cede their western territories to them so that new states could be formed that would later join the confederation. It was one of the few beneficial things that they were able to accomplish during this period.

The average person was affected by the severe economic conditions caused by war and the limited access to economic factors that were available before the problems with Britain began. There were accusations that a select group of businessmen were profiting from the war at the expense of others. Raphael (2002) claimed that militia in Philadelphia "seized over twenty wealthy men who they accused of profiteering and threw them in jail" while others were able to "turn the sentiments of the lower classes into a genuine social movement" that "threatened a revolution within the Revolution" (p. 123).

There were also other issues of inequity that potentially threatened the outcome of the independence movement. Raphael (2002) stated that objections to the drafting of men were prevalent as "the rich could buy their way out, the poor could not" (p. 187). Others were taken advantage of due to their lack of education or skills. Some places like New York had citizens who had "become indifferent, if not averse, to a Government which in place of the Liberty Prosperity safety and Plenty ... has established a thorough Despotism" (Raphael, 2002, p. 219).

The abolition movement continued to gain momentum in the northern states. Massachusetts and Pennsylvania joined Vermont (not yet a state) in banning slavery in their states. Women, meanwhile, struggled to have an impact on the war but were affected by the dismal economic conditions as well. Raphael (2002) mentioned that a 1778 army memo said "the wimen [sic] grumble at the price of shirts – make the best bargain you can with them" (p. 147).

*Set 9 Perceived Task Complexity.* James Madison wrote to Jefferson in 1780 that the public Treasury was empty, the capital markets were "exhausted," and a sense among the citizens of each state that they were victims of extortion from taxes and levies aimed at paying for the war (Cunningham, 1987, p. 67). This period of time may be defined as the darkest one of the Revolutionary War. The score for this period was 3.00.

*Set 9 Structural Leadership Profile.* John Jay served as President of the Continental Congress for 10 months in 1779. Samuel Huntington was then elected and served through the end of the period. Not much is known about his personal profile so the actions of Congress under his watch were considered to be fairly consistent with his and, as such, were used to fill out the instrument. Congress struggled to gain control over some aspects of the confederation but were still cautious so as not to be viewed as usurping power. The calculation of leader weights can be found in Table 5.

Table 5 - Calculation of weights for set 9 multiple influential leaders

| Leader number, n | Leader name | Influence time, m (in months / 24) | Time factor, t (m/24*0.5) | Magnitude / Scope, s (from little - 1 - to great - 3) | Mag. / scope factor, f (s/3*0.5) | Sum of factors, x (t+f) | Weight, w (x / sum of x's) |
|---|---|---|---|---|---|---|---|
| 1 | John Jay | 10 | 0.2083333 | 1 | 0.16666667 | 0.375 | 0.45 |
| 2 | S. Huntington | 14 | 0.2916667 | 1 | 0.16666667 | 0.458333 | 0.55 |
| | | | | | Sum: | 0.833333 | 1 |

John Jay's score was 3.30 and Samuel Huntingtons's was 3.70. The two scores were calculated using the weighted values to give a score for this period of 3.53.

*Set 9 Structural Followership Profile.* The followers of this period included soldiers, women, loyalists, and common citizens who began to feel the heavy burden of war and economic malaise. George Washington's influence among followers continued to grow as his attempts to hold the army together and his occasional victories gave the citizens something to be hopeful about. He increasingly became frustrated with the consensus approach to solving national problems. Many followers began to realize that a strong leader may be necessary to take control of environmental aspects in order to make it through the difficult times. Their views were summarized and resulted in a score for the set of 3.19. The congruence was 0.35

*Set 9 Social Satisfaction Instrument.* The lack of clear American battlefield victories and the inability of citizens to adequately provide for themselves, let alone an army, affected the prevailing satisfaction for this period. The trend toward dissatisfaction with Congress continued. Turnover in the Continental Congress was 47.4%. The score for this period was 2.25.

*Set 10: 1781-1782.*

The years in Set 10 began with the deepening despair present at the end of Set 9. The Continental Army experienced a continued lack of supplies and low morale. The tide began to turn with some key American battlefield victories and the signing of a preliminary peace treaty with the British. A new superintendent of finance worked diligently to restore the weak economy to some level that could provide what the Americans needed.

The lack of supplies and pay increased the level of dissatisfaction among soldiers in early 1781. George Washington (1997) put the situation this way:

> The aggravated calamities and distresses that have resulted, from the total want of pay for nearly twelve Months, for want of cloathing [*sic*], at a severe season, and not unfrequently the want of provisions; are beyond description (p. 407).

Pennsylvania troops mutinied in New Jersey but were prevented from getting out of control by Massachusetts troops under the command of General Robert Howe. Washington ordered the execution of two of the leaders for inciting the action and it was said in the General Orders written by a staff officer in January 1781 that he was "happy in the lenity shewn [*sic*] in the execution of only two of the most guilty after compelling the whole to an unconditional surrender, and he flatters himself no similar instance will hereafter disgrace our military History" (Washington, 1997, p. 416).

Additional issues of paper currency only destabilized the economy more. Congress took steps to improve the condition of the economy by selecting Robert Morris to be the Superintendent of Finance. Schlesinger (1993) stated that "through his extensive reorganization efforts and forthcoming loans and aid from France and the Netherlands, Morris is able to make some progress by the end of the year" (p. 133). Morris, heavily influenced by Alexander Hamilton, proposed the creation of the Bank of North America as a means to regulate currency and its impact on consumers, businesses, and government. It was chartered and came into existence on December 31, 1781.

Congress had success in another area that affected the economy and the satisfaction of Americans. Maryland became the last state to ratify the Articles of Confederation in March of 1781. The new confederation of states was based on:

> a firm league of friendship with each other, for their common defence [*sic*],
>
> the security of their liberties, and their mutual and general welfare, binding
>
> themselves to assist each other, against all force offered to, or attacks made
>
> upon them, on account of religion, sovereignty, trade, or any other pretense
>
> whatever (Ketcham, 1986, p. 357).

The new name of Congress changed from The Continental Congress to The United States Congress Assembled. A stronger sense of unity had a reinforcing effect on many Americans. Samuel Huntington continued to be President of Congress until July 1781 when Thomas McKean of Delaware was elected. John Hanson of Maryland was elected in November of 1781 and served as President through the end of the period.

Spring brought a new round of fighting as both sides emerged from winter quarters. There were roughly equal wins and losses for both sides but the most significant battle began in late September 1781 in Yorktown. When it was over British General Cornwallis surrendered to American and French forces. Washington (1997) wrote to President Thomas McKean that he had "the Honor to inform Congress, that a Reduction of the British Army under the Command of Lord Cornwallis, is most happily effected" and he praised every officer and soldier for the result (p. 454 – 465).

The victory at Yorktown was so profound that it was one of the reasons the British Parliament voted four months later to end the war and begin peace negotiations.

Congress had earlier appointed John Adams, John Jay, Benjamin Franklin, Henry Laurens and Thomas Jefferson to negotiate a peace settlement of which the main American demand was complete independence from Britain. The negotiations continued throughout 1782 that ended in November 1782 with the signing of a preliminary peace treaty. The treaty included:

> British recognition of American independence, the specific boundaries of the
>
> United States territory, continued American fishing rights off the coast of eastern
>
> Canada, a validation of debts, a restoration of rights and property to American
>
> Loyalists, and the withdrawal of British forces from American territory
>
> (Schlesinger, 1993, p. 136).

The last major conflict between American and British forces occurred in August near the Combahee River in South Carolina while fighting between Americans and loyalists continued through November.

The loyalists began to leave America in large numbers in 1782 as they feared reprisals by citizens and the government as a result of their support for the British. A Board of Associated Loyalists assisted many in leaving for places like Nova Scotia and East Florida. Raphael (2002) added that at seaports "thousands of homeless refugees vied with each other for limited shelter, many having to settle for tents" as they waited their turn to leave "with over 9,000 leaving Charleston at the end of 1782" (p. 225).

Other aspects that affected the environment included the restoration of fishing rights for New Englanders, a large loan package that John Adams had negotiated with Holland, and the cessation of hostilities between America and Britain. The loan package was very important because "it was money desperately needed at home and a foundation for American credit in Europe" (McCullough, 2001, p. 272). There was hope that trade would be quickly restored between the two countries. 1782 marked the point at which a young and soon to be very influential American, Alexander Hamilton, left the services of General Washington and was elected to Congress as a representative of New York. He was an advocate of a strong central government and a central banking system as means to restore and maintain stability.

*Set 10 Perceived Task Complexity.* The environment was in a dire situation at the beginning of this period. Inflation was rampant due to too much of the worthless Continental currency in circulation. Trade was still at such a low level that most goods that one needed either had to be produced locally or not at all. Things took a change for the better as the months progressed due to the stabilization of the economy, the increase of trade with France and the Netherlands, and a tentative peace treaty. The score for this period remained at 3.08.

*Set 10 Structural Leadership Profile.* Samuel Huntington was President of Congress for 6 months, Thomas McKean for 4 months, John Hanson of Maryland for 12 months, and Elias Boudinot of New Jersey for 2 months. There was little information on specific actions for each of these individuals nor were there much on their personalities and other defining criteria. The actions of Congress were analyzed in place of each one's individual aspects in order to determine leadership of the period. Some of the members began to realize that allowing the states too much power prevented the accomplishment of many essential tasks. A lack of coordination among all states caused some activities such as feeding the army to come to a halt. The score for the combined Presidents was 3.40.

*Set 10 Structural Followership Profile.* Many of the Continental soldiers were very upset at the miserable conditions they encountered on a regular basis. The fact that they were trying to defend a country that appeared indifferent toward the soldier's problems infuriated many to commit mutiny. Despite this many found George Washington to be the only person that kept them together. He provided discipline and care that they could not obtain from Congress and the states. It appeared that a certain level of government was required in order to ensure some satisfactory level of happiness. Loyalists, sensing that there was no room for them in an independent country began to leave to find better living conditions. The score for this set was 3.19. The degree of congruence was 0.10.

*Set 10 Social Satisfaction Instrument.* The dismal living conditions for the troops and the poor economy gradually gave way to prospects for a better future as a result of a tentative peace deal and efforts taken to stabilize and improve economic conditions. New trading partners would soon provide markets to both buy needed goods and sell American products. The view toward Congress was mixed to dissatisfied as it appeared that it was incapable of accomplishing many tasks. Turnover in the Continental Congress increased to 57%. The score for this period dropped slightly to 2.14.

*Set 11: 1783-1784.*

The end of hostilities and a finalized peace treaty promised to return prosperity and happiness to the Americans. Many foreign governments recognized the independence of the United States and efforts were made to establish beneficial trade agreements. Dissatisfaction was still evident as loyalists completed a mass emigration and soldiers, both former and present, struggled to get Congress to deliver on its promises to them. It was also a time for an effective leader, Washington, to leave the scene for a new group.

Early in 1783 the British announced that they had ordered an end to all fighting in America. A tentative agreement had been reached in Paris a few short months ago while both sides continued to finalize the agreement. The Treaty of Paris was signed in September of 1783, officially bringing the war to an end. The last British troops left New York City on December 4, 1783.

America gained new recognition in the international community with the official acknowledgment of its independence by Spain, Sweden, Denmark, and Russia. The task was left to John Adams, Benjamin Franklin, and Thomas Jefferson in Europe to try to negotiate trade agreements with the countries there in order to revitalize the American economy. They are met with limited success as England agreed to import American goods on favorable terms while trade with China was starting to take off. This success was countered by the closure of the West Indies by Britain in 1783 and the lower Mississippi River by Spain in 1784 to Americans. An act of Congress created the Treasury Board to replace the Superintendent of Finance in an effort to further assist the economic recovery.

The war had ended but the soldiers were still unhappy. Raphael (2002) stated that "throughout the war they had been told to wait until the end; now the end had arrived" and they were still waiting" (p. 127). Washington and Alexander Hamilton both warned Congress that if they failed to provide for the soldiers there would be serious consequences. Washington (1997) told Hamilton that "the danger, to which the Army

has been exposed, to a political dissolution for want of subsistence .... would at this day

be productive of Civil commotions & end in blood" (p. 488). Hamilton replied in a later

letter that "if the army was not properly compensated after peace was declared, the

soldiers would use their bayonets to procure justice, with or without General

Washington" (Langguth, 1988, p. 558).

The first sign of discontent appeared among Washington's officers in New York.

An anonymous letter, known as the Newburgh Address, was circulated among the

officers that admonished "Congress for the failure to honor its promises to Continental

Army soldiers and [exhorted] the veterans to defy Congress" if they were not

compensated soon (Schlesinger, 1993, p. 137). Washington immediately issued a

General Order that banned all unapproved meetings and set up a meeting with select

officers to address their concerns. He then wrote to President Elias Boudinot to inform

him that he would continue to "promote the welfare" of the United States "under the most

lively Expectation, that Congress have the best Intentions of doing ample Justice to the

Army, as soon as Circumstances will possibly admit" (Washington, 1997, p. 496). A

speech to his officers that called on them to moderate their actions and keep in mind

posterity's view of their actions, along with a distinguished yet subtle personal plea from

Washington, succeeded in holding off mutinous action.

A few months later a group of veterans approach Philadelphia, where Congress

was sitting, with the same complaints. This time the threat the soldiers presented caused

Congress to flee for their safety to Princeton, New Jersey. Alexander Hamilton "was

often the servant of Congress in dealing with military affairs" due to "his war experience and, particularly, because of his knowledge of army administration." (Mitchell, 1999, p. 125). The Pennsylvania militia was supposed to provide security and should have been able to put down the mutiny but was ill-equipped to do so. Hamilton and Washington ordered a detachment from West Point to put down the mutiny, which happened before the soldiers arrived. The affair reinforced Hamilton's view that reliance on states effectively meant a weak central government.

Hamilton and Washington were the most vocal in their views about problems with the current system of government. Washington (1997), in a letter to Hamilton, stated that "no man in the United States is, or can be more deeply impressed with the necessity of a reform in our present Confederation than myself" (p. 505). A letter was sent to all of the states by Washington in June of 1783 that suggested that one federal head, equality of all through a justice system, an effective army for defense and peace, and the removal of prejudices were necessary in order for the union to survive. Failure to address these issues meant that domestic aspects "must very rapidly tend to Anarchy and confusion" and then from anarchy to tyranny (Washington, 1997, pp. 519 - 520).

Washington decided though that he wanted to return to private life. He bid farewell to his officers on December 4, 1783 in New York City where he tearfully thanked them all for their service to the country. The final farewell address to Congress included the resignation of his commission as commander in chief of the army and a request that Congress take care of the soldiers. Alexander Hamilton stood ready to assume the role of public advocate where Washington left off.

Other notable events included the continued exodus of loyalists and more examples of movement toward abolition of slavery in the northern states. Loyalists completed a mass emigration from America in 1783 with the departure of the last British troops. The total number of loyalists that left was estimated at 100,000. Many state and local governments had confiscated loyalist property to help pay for the war among other things. One of the conditions of the Treaty of Paris was that seized loyalist property was to be returned to the rightful owners. This last item continued to be an area of contention between the Americans and British.

The abolition of slavery in the north was furthered by legislative action in Connecticut and Rhode Island to abolish slavery and court cases in Massachusetts that accomplished the same end. The Virginia House of Burgesses passed legislation in October of 1783 that freed all slaves who served in the Continental Army.

*Set 11 Perceived Task Complexity.* The environment began to improve for the first time in quite a while as the war ended, international recognition and the trade associated with it, and the efforts of Congress to improve general economic conditions helped restore viability to the economy. The main hindrance was a weak central government and indecisive states that limited cooperation and a unified approach to aspects that would benefit the nation as a whole. The score for this period was 3.17.

*Set 11 Structural Leadership Profile.* Elias Boudinot was President of Congress for 2 months, Thomas Mifflin of Pennsylvania for 13 months, and Richard Henry Lee of Virginia for one month during this set. None of the Presidents stood out or had extensive histories that could be effectively used to construct individual profiles. A weak Congress was unable to provide a relatively strong degree of leadership. The score for the Presidents was 3.65.

*Set 11 Structural Followership Profile.* The views of the followers were expressed by the soldiers as they struggled to get Congress to compensate them for their services. Washington and Hamilton were increasingly the voice of reason among the followers. The continued abolitionist movement in north provided some insight into how others were viewed by Americans in that part of the country. Loyalists completed their exodus as they feared retaliation. The score for this set was 3.13. The degree of congruence was 0.35.

*Set 11 Social Satisfaction Instrument.* The lack of compensation for soldiers weighed heavily on social satisfaction. The mutiny in Philadelphia showed that the federal government was truly bound by the states and their indecisiveness. Dissatisfaction with Congress stemmed from its relative inability to accomplish significant tasks. Turnover in the Continental Congress increased to 82.6%. The score for this period was 2.85.

*Set 12: 1785-1786.*

The war was over and America tried to put itself back together politically and economically. The difficulties encountered when trying to raise revenue to pay war debts and to get all states to agree on a common set of objectives forced various parties to demand something better. Efforts to improve the economy met with limited success and a fair amount of failures.

The first attempt of this set to create improvements in the current system of federal government was in January when Congress selected James Madison to get the states to cede some of their power to it in order to make it easier to regulate overseas trade. It was not successful so states began to make deals with each other to accomplish similar tasks. A conference at Mount Vernon produced an agreement between Virginia

and Maryland that focused on uniform currency and trade between them. Other states

were invited to attend in January of 1786 by Virginia. A second attempt was a resolution

in the Massachusetts assembly recommended revisions to the Articles of Confederation.

Schlesinger (1993) suggested that, although it was never delivered to Congress "its

passage [marked] the growing recognition of the individual states that a stronger central

government [was] needed if the new nation [was] to survive and prosper" (p. 140).

Tax collections from the states to pay for debt reduction and national government

operations were sporadic and difficult to enforce. New Jersey refused to send its share of

taxes to Congress in 1786 which magnified the "weaknesses of the Articles of

Confederation (Schlesinger, 1993, p. 141). Various committees were formed by

Congress to look at solutions, including amendments to the Articles that would

strengthen the powers of Congress, but they were either not acted on or presented to the

states for fear that they would not be accepted. Washington (1997) wryly commented

that it was "a triumph for the advocates of despotism to find that we are incapable of

governing ourselves, and that systems founded on the basis of equal liberty are merely

ideal & fallacious" (p. 606).

Another unsuccessful attempt to get the states to work out their differences led

Alexander Hamilton to call for a convention to revise the current system of government.

Hamilton laid out to the states all of the defects of the current system and what the future

held if things were not changed. The final statement was Hamilton's recommendation

that every state send delegates to:

Philadelphia on the second Monday in May next, to take into consideration the situation of the United States, to devise such further provis:ons as shall appear to

them necessary to rend the constitution of the Foederal [*sic*] Government,

adequate to the exigencies of the Union (Mitchell, 1999, p. 144).

The call for a convention was reviewed by Congress and recommend in early 1787.

Washington (1997) wrote that he "scarcely [knew] what opinion to entertain of a general

Convention" and added "that it [was] necessary to revise, and amend the articles of

Confederation" but the "consequences of such an attempt" were doubtful (p. 600).

There were other signs of discontent, especially in New England. A statewide

meeting of town delegates was held to "consider the problems resu:ting from economic

depression that were not addressed by the latest session of the Massachusetts legislature –

the steadily increasing number of farm and home foreclosures, and the popular calls for a

paper-money issue" (Schlesinger, 1993, p. 141). Paper money was a particular problem

as each state issued its own and there was no uniformity. A state court in Rhode Island

ruled that "forcing a creditor to accept paper money in payment of a debt [was]

unconstitutional" because it was inconsistent with the state's property guarantee

(Schlesinger, 1993, p. 141). Other states printed money as well at :he urging of their

citizens in order to pay debts.

All were affected in one way or another by debts, attempts :o collect taxes, seizure

of property for nonpayment of either, and economic hardships. Raphael (2002) offered a

poem by Hannah Griffitts written in 1785 as an example of the frustration many felt:

The glorious fourth – again appears

A Day of Days – and year of years,

The sum of sad disasters,

Where all the mighty gains we see

With all their Boasted liberty,

Is only Change of Masters (p. 391).

An armed band of farmers that felt the same way descended on the supreme court in Springfield, Massachusetts in protest of their plight. Congress requested troops from Connecticut and Massachusetts to go a nearby arsenal and prevent its seizure by the mob. The conflict that ensued came to be known as Shays' Rebellion and was eventually put down by state troops. It was the most dramatic display yet of problems that needed to be resolved. James Madison thought that the rebellion was "a crisis in civil government and feared the Confederation was 'tottering to its foundation'" while Jefferson, who took an opposing view, wrote "God forbid we should ever be 20 years without such a rebellion" because he felt such actions were healthy (Cunningham, 1987, p. 116). John Adams had a similar different view when he told Jefferson not to "be alarmed at the late turbulence in New England" because Massachusetts had "in its zeal to get the better of their debt, laid a tax rather heavier than the people could bear" and the result of the rebellion would "terminate in additional strength to the government" (McCullough, 2001, pp. 368-369). Washington (1997) felt that such actions were "one of the evils of democratical governments that the people, not always seeing & frequently mislead, must often feel before they can act right" to bring about a better system (p. 595). Content followers did not force change unless they were personally affected.

Attempts to improve economic conditions were intermeshed with political conditions. James Madison suggested that "most of our political evils may be traced up to our commercial ones" (Mitchell, 1999, p. 141). Congress appointed people like John Jay and John Adams to negotiate trade deals with other nations that would be beneficial to America. Jay was not successful in getting the Spanish to grant navigation of the Mississippi to America while Adams was able to get Prussia to agree to a trade pact. Adams tried unsuccessfully to negotiate a settlement that would eliminate the piracy off the coast of Africa that was harming American shipping. Meanwhile, many states imposed "discriminatory tariffs to encourage the development of American domestic industry" (Schlesinger, 1993, p. 140). A new coinage system and the founding of the U.S. mint also occurred during this period. Schlesinger (1993) added that the prevailing depression reached "a low point, caused by currency shortages, high taxes and persistent creditors" as well as all of the "unstable paper currency" in existence in all of the states (p. 141).

*Set 12 Perceived Task Complexity.* There were some successes with trade agreements that opened up international markets from which Americans could buy and sell products. The lack of uniformity between states with respect to trade and currency hindered any serious economic reforms. High and inconsistent taxes combined with poor economic growth kept expectations low and essential economic resources from being utilized to their best. The score for this set was 2.83.

*Set 12 Structural Leadership Profile.* John Hancock was President of Congress for 5 months, Nathaniel Gorham of Massachusetts for 8 months, and Arthur St. Clair of Pennsylvania for 11 months. There was sufficient information to fill out an instrument but insufficient for the other two. The actions of Congress, as in other sets, were used to fill out the instrument for Gorham and St. Clair. Congress was faced with an environment where individual states did their own thing with little regard for a national focus. The failures of this approach became more apparent toward the end of the set as many vocal citizens began to call for changes. The weights for each are found in Table 6.

Table 6 - Calculation of weights for set 12 multiple influential leaders

| Leader number, n | Leader name | Influence time, m (in months / 24) | Time factor, t (m/24*0.5) | Magnitude / Scope, s (from little - 1 - to great - 3) | Mag. / scope factor, f (s/3*0.5) | Sum of factors, x (t+f) | Weight, w (x / sum of x's) |
|---|---|---|---|---|---|---|---|
| 1 | John Hancock | 5 | 0.1041667 | 1 | 0.16666667 | 0.270833 | 0.325 |
| 2 | Presidents | 19 | 0.3958333 | 1 | 0.16666667 | 0.5625 | 0.675 |
| | | | | | Sum: | 0.833333 | 1 |

The score for John Hancock was 3.45 while the score for the Presidents was 3.55. The calculated score for this set was 3.52.

*Set 12 Structural Followership Profile.* Farmers and merchants were the most vocal during this set. John Adams, Thomas Jefferson, James Madison, George Washington, and Alexander Hamilton provided examples of what people thought. The score for this set was 3.13. The calculation of congruence was 0.46.

*Set 12 Social Satisfaction Instrument.* Bankruptcies, property seizures, and rebellions were signs of social satisfaction. The increased calls for change were also an indication that the system of national government was not ideal for the needs of Americans. The turnover for Congress was 90.3% as only 5 original members remained at the end of 1786. The score for this period was 3.11.

*Set 13: 1787-1788.*

Shays' Rebellion was suppressed and 12 of the 13 states sent delegates to the Constitutional Convention. A new Constitution was approved by Congress and sent to each state to vote on approval. The end of 1788 was the last time Congress, under the Articles of Confederation, met as the new government under the approved Constitution was to take office in April of 1789.

Daniel Shays led an unsuccessful attack on the federal arsenal at Springfield, Massachusetts in January. The rebellion was over by the end of January and amnesty was offered to all participants except for Shays and a few other leaders. Schlesinger (1993) suggested that "this rebellion [had] the result of causing the state legislature to avoid direct taxation, to lower court costs, and to exempt household necessities and workmen's tools from the debt process" (p. 142). There were mixed views regarding the rebellion as people like Jefferson and, to an extent, Adams felt that events like the rebellion were healthy for a country while Madison and Washington were concerned about the breakdown in government that could result. Washington (1997) wrote to Secretary of War Henry Know that "if government shrinks, or is unable to enforce its laws; fresh manoeuvres [sic] will be displayed by the insurgents – anarchy & confusion must prevail – and every thing will be turned topsy turvey in that State" (p. 634).

George Washington was selected President of the Constitutional Convention that also included people like Benjamin Franklin, Alexander Hamilton, James Madison, and Roger Sherman of Connecticut. Rhode Island was the only state not to participate in the convention. The first alternative to be proposed was known as the Virginia Plan as it was offered by Edmund Randolph of Virginia. Ketcham (1986) stated that "the plan embodied Madison's intention to greatly strengthen the national government, and boldly set out to frame an entirely new constitution rather than simply amend the Articles of Confederation as the Convention was formally charged to do" (p. 35). Randolph enumerated the defects of the current system and then proposed that a new government should have a legislature with two branches, one house's members elected by the people and the other nominated by each state's legislature, a federal executive selected by the federal legislative branch, and a judiciary appointed in the same manner. The debate on this plan began on May 31 as Elbridge Gerry of Massachusetts told the convention that "the evils we experience flow from the excess of democracy" and George Mason of Virginia "admitted that we had been too democratic but was afraid we should incautiously run into the opposite extreme" (Ketcham, 1986, pp. 39-40).

An alternative known as the New Jersey Plan was offered on June 15 by William Paterson. This plan was not as radical as the Virginia Plan in that it called only for modifications to the existing Articles of Confederation to allow for a plurality of executives, more taxing power for the legislature, and a federal court system. The main backers of this plan were the small states because they were concerned that the larger states would have more power than they did. Alexander Hamilton rose to say that "real liberty is neither found in despotism or the extremes of democracy, but in moderate governments .... if we incline too much to democracy, we shall soon shoot into a monarchy" (Mitchell, 1999, p. 153). Lengthy debate followed that focused mainly on the equal representation of states on one side of the argument and proportional representation on the other side and ended when seven states voted to table the plan and return to the Virginia Plan.

A compromise was offered on July 16 by Roger Sherman of Connecticut that provided for equal representation in the upper house and proportional representation in the lower house. Debate then moved to how the executive would be selected, either by the legislature or the public at large. Roger Sherman was concerned that the public "will never be sufficiently informed of characters, and besides will never give a majority of votes to any one man" (Ketcham, 1986, p. 114). Governeur Morris claimed that "if the Executive be chosen by the National Legislature, he will not be independent of it; and if not independent, usurpation and tyranny on the part of the Legislature will be the consequence" (Ketcham, 1986, pp. 115-116). A final resolution of the convention was to avoid the slave issue for 20 years.

September 17 was the day the Constitution was signed by all attendants with the exception of Edmund Randolph, George Mason, and Elbridge Gerry. It was then sent to Congress for ratification by George Washington who added that it was "the result of a spirit of amity, and of that mutual deference and concession which the peculiarity of our political situation rendered indispensable" (Washington, 1997, p. 655). Congress approved the Constitution on September 28 and forwarded it to the states for ratification.

What followed was a period of intense public debate as to the benefits and weaknesses of the proposed Constitution. James Madison, Alexander Hamilton, and John Jay wrote many articles for newspapers that began in1787 and continued through 1788 and focused on the merits of the Constitution. There was a large amount of concern that a republican government would be worse than a democracy because more liberties were given up. Madison, in Federalist 14 written November 30, 1787, tried to allay those fears when he stated that "in a democracy the people meet and exercise the government in person; in a republic they assemble and administer it by their representatives and agents" (Kesler, 1961, p. 68). Democracies only worked when the geographic area was small but in the case of America the area was too large.

Alexander Hamilton, in Federalist 15 written in early December, pointed out the some of the faults of the current government. He tried to tie the poor economic conditions, the inability to obtain favorable trade conditions, and the weak view other nations had of America to the inabilities of Congress to address them. Hamilton added that "we may indeed with propriety be said to have reached almost the last stage of national humiliation" (Kesler, 1961, p. 74). It was also suggested that the good intentions of representatives or agents who represented each state could not be counted on because of human nature.

John Jay, in Federalists 2 through 5 beginning in late October, argued that foreign and domestic threats called for a stronger federal government. Jay said that "the safety of the people of America against dangers from *foreign* force depends not only on their forbearing to give *just* causes of war to other nations, but also on their placing and continuing themselves in such a situation as not to *invite* hostility or insult" (Kesler, 1961, p. 14). The past experiences of Shays' Rebellion and other mob violence and the inability of the states or federal government to adequately respond created impressions in foreign governments that America was weak. The result was that Spain closed the Mississippi and Britain continued to occupy American territory that they were supposed to evacuate at the end of the war.

Federalist 84, written in May of 1788 by Hamilton, attempted to address miscellaneous concerns of the Anti-Federalists. A big concern of theirs was the lack of a bill of rights. Hamilton suggested that this was not as big a deal as they made it because "the constitutions of several of the States are in a similar predicament" (Kesler, 1961, p. 478). The current Constitution offered protections to citizens such as trial by jury, the charge of treason only for waging war against American, and the prohibition of ex post facto laws. He also added that the "bill of rights, in the sense and to the extent in which they are contended for, are not only unnecessary in the proposed Constitution but would even be dangerous" (Kesler, 1961, p. 481). He meant that by claiming specific rights when nothing in the Constitution specifically stated that there was a reason to be concerned about it may create precedence for manipulation of implied powers.

The Anti-Federalists included people like John Dewitt, a fictional name of a Massachusetts farmer, and Patrick Henry. They believed that by "retaining as much [power] as possible the vitality of local government where rulers and ruled could see, know, and understand each other" was a better system of government (Ketcham, 1986, p. 17). John Dewitt wrote two essays in October of 1787 that cautioned against a speedy ratification and the lack of a bill of rights. Dewitt stated that "every man is a TRAITOR to himself and his posterity, who shall ratify it with his signature, without first endeavouring [sic] to understand it" (Ketcham, 1986, p. 192). It was better to take the time to read, understand, and determine the outcomes of such a system of government before accepting it. A second essay focused on the fact that the system of government proposed in the Constitution could not be revised every year and as such could not be altered except by force. This condition thus required a bill of rights to declare rights of individuals and the route by which change could be initiated.

Patrick Henry gave two speeches to the Virginia Ratifying Convention in June of 1788 that expressed his concerns about the Constitution. Henry first stated that the current system of government was fine because "it carried us through a long and dangerous war .... and secured us a territory greater than any European Monarch possesses" (Ketcham, 1986, p. 201). He was more concerned about tyranny by the minority. His argument was that the smaller states with the least amount of population could hold the majority of the country hostage because of the three-fourths requirement for passage of amendments. Henry felt that when "amendments are left to the twentieth or the tenth part of the people of America, your liberty is gone forever" (Ketcham, 1986, p. 205). Taxation was always a sore spot for Henry and he displayed it as well in this situation by stating that Virginians could be taxed by a minority that had no connection to them.

Delaware was the first state to ratify the Constitution, Pennsylvania was second, and New Jersey third to finish out 1787. New Hampshire was the ninth state to accept the Constitution and thus brought it into force. Rhode Island rejected it while New York and Virginia did not approve it until it was already approved by the majority of states. The concern of the reluctant states was a lack of a bill of rights, of which 12 amendments were submitted to the states on September 28, 1788.

The last President of Congress under the Articles of Confederation, Cyrus Griffin, announced on July 2, 1788 that the Constitution was now the basis of the new government. November 1 was the last day that the old Congress met and the nation would not have a sitting government until the new Congress under the Constitution met for the first time in April of 1789. The economy improved at the end of 1788 as "a continuing downward plunge in commodity prices [was] finally halted, thus paving the way for the reinstatement of pre-Revolutionary prosperity" (Schlesinger, 1993, p. 152).

*Set 13 Perceived Task Complexity.* The environment remained mired in an economic depression that was sustained by an ineffective Congress and the lack of uniformity between the states. A large amount of time for this set was consumed by the Constitutional Convention and the ratification process. Ratification of the Constitution helped bring an end to the economic problems and instilled confidence in Americans that things were going to be better. The score for this period, 3.00, included the dismal conditions early on and the better conditions at the end.

*Set 13 Structural Leadership Profile.* Nathaniel Gorham was President for 1 month, Arthur St. Clair of Pennsylvania was President for 12 months, and Cyrus Griffin of Virginia was President for the next 11 months. The actions of Congress were utilized to fill out the instruments, as in past sets, because there was little information on any of these individuals. The score for this set was 3.55.

*Set 13 Structural Followership Profile.* The rebellious farmers, the Constitutional Convention delegates, and the propagandist Federalists and Anti-Federalists were typical of the followers of this period. It was they who were able to successfully bring about a new government that they hoped would accomplish the goals of security and prosperity without infringing on their liberties. The score for this set was 3.13. The degree of congruence was 0.37.

*Set 13 Social Satisfaction Instrument.* The dismal economic conditions led farmers and others to riot. The perceived inabilities of Congress were the stimulus to search for and implement a new form of government. The fact that it was brought about in a peaceful manner was a hallmark of history. The turnover in Congress was 78.7%. The score for this set was 2.67.

*Set 14: 1789-1790.*

A new government that operated under the new Constitution began in this set. A new President, Congress, and Supreme Court began the task of ensuring progress toward the two objectives of prosperity and freedom.

Massachusetts and Rhode Island, the last two holdouts in the Constitution ratification process, finally voted to ratify it in 1789 and 1790 respectively. The proposed amendments to the Constitution were the primary reasons that they finally agreed to accept it. New Jersey became the first state to ratify the Bill of Rights in 1789.

The 1st Congress convened on March 4, 1789 but lacked sufficient numbers to achieve a quorum so they had to wait until April 1. The presidential ballots were counted in the Senate on April 6 with George Washington elected President as all 69 votes were cast for him. John Adams was elected Vice President with 34 votes. Washington (1997) gave his Inaugural Address on April 30, in which he closed by saying:

> I shall take my present leave; but not without resorting once more to the benign
>
> Parent of the human race, in humble supplication that since he has been pleased to
>
> favour [*sic*] the American people, with opportunities for deliberating in perfect
>
> tranquility, and dispositions for deciding with unparellelled [*sic*] unanimity on a
>
> form of Government, for the security of their Union, and the advancement of
>
> their happiness; so this divine blessing may be equally *conspicuous* in the
>
> enlarged views – the temperate consultations, and the wise measures on which
>
> the success of this Government must depend (p. 734).

There was speculation that the address was written all or in part by James Madison.

Congress set to work passing laws to fund and run essential tasks of the
government. There was the Tariff Act which placed a tax of 8.5 percent on selected
imports unless they were shipped on American ships, which were then granted a 10
percent reduction. A similar measure, the Tonnage Act, placed a tax of 50 cents per ton
on any non-American ship that brought cargo into or out of American ports. The
Departments of State, War, and Treasury were authorized and staffed by Thomas
Jefferson, Henry Knox, and Alexander Hamilton respectively. The Federal Judiciary Act
was passed in September of 1789 which created a Supreme Court with a Chief Justice
and five Associates, an Attorney General, 13 district courts, and 3 circuit courts of
appeals. John Jay was nominated as Chief Justice and Edmund Randolph as Attorney
General. Proposed amendments to the Constitution were sent to the states for ratification.
An army and Revenue Marine Service were established and the Census Act, which called
for a periodic census, was passed.

The view of the new government was positive even among those who were very
dissatisfied with the last one. George Washington (1997) felt that "the Government,
though not absolutely perfect, is one of the best in the World" and added that "the
harvests of Wheat have been remarkably good – the demand for that article from abroad
is great – the encrease [sic] of Commerce is visible in every Port – and the number of
new Manufactures introduced in one year is astounding ' (pp. 752-753). Thomas
Jefferson was concerned how the rest of the world viewed the new republic. He was
unsure whether he wanted to accept the job as Secretary of State but did so because "a
new government struggling to establish itself under the Constitution" that had "set the

example for mankind" should not be perceived as weak because a given person did not want to accept a senior position in it (Cunningham, 1987, p. 134).

Washington was aware of the precedence that he was setting so he kept an eye on the future implications of his actions. The way he viewed his cabinet was one of "assistants, not as independent ministers" as he sought out their advice but "he made it clear that he was in charge of his administration and expected that all policy matters be presented to him for approval" (Cunningham, 1987, p. 137). John Adams was also aware of the precedents that were set. A lively discussion began in the Senate, of which Adams was presiding officer, about how to address the President. McCullough (2001) suggested that "Adams believed everything possible should be done to bring dignity and respect to the central government and thus strengthen the union" (p. 405). The final title was President of the United States.

A major disagreement emerged as to how the debt of the states and international obligations should be handled. Alexander Hamilton wanted the federal government to assume all debt in order to establish a uniform and consistent credit history among all market participants. It began with Hamilton's submission of the *Report on the Public Credit* which laid out his goal of assuming all debt held by citizens at par value. Ellis (2000) said that "what began to trouble Madison, then terrify him, was not Hamilton's goal – the recovery of public credit –but the way he proposed to reach it" (p. 55). Madison was concerned that soldiers who were paid with debt and had sold them at heavily discounted prices when the economy was in shambles would be cheated. He also was worried that the speculation in the bonds would enrich a small class of citizens while shortchanging the rest. Another concern was that the assumption would be unfair to

Virginia because it had paid a large share of its debt while heavily indebted northern

states would greatly benefit. The final problem that Madison had was that he felt that the

federal debt would require higher taxes and an increase in federal power over the states.

A compromise was reached at a dinner between Jefferson, Madison, and

Hamilton. Jefferson brought Madison and Hamilton together and indicated to Hamilton

that the south would need something to compensate them for the perceived unfairness of

the assumption. The proposal was to build the new federal capital on land between

Virginia and Maryland. Ellis (2000) suggested that Jefferson liked this idea because he

was fearful of the concentration of power in a given area (p. 79). New York and

Philadelphia were the centers of commerce and financial power in America so it was

probably more satisfying that the political capital would be in the south. Despite

continued opposition led by Patrick Henry Congress approved Hamilton's plan for debt

assumption. Hamilton also submitted a proposal for a Bank of the United States to

facilitate the assumption process.

The revolution in France was followed closely by Americans. The issues that

were at the forefront of the revolution were the same ones the Americans faced not only

with the British but during the Constitutional Convention and ratification process. An

influential book by Edmund Burke, a British politician, highlighted many of the views

Americans held. Burke was concerned that revolutions like the one in France could

quickly spin out of control. McCullough (2001) added that "the French, said Burke,

sounding very much like Adams, had 'destroyed all balances and counterpoises which

serve to fix a state and give it steady direction, and then they melted down the whole into

one incongruous mass of mob and democracy'" (p. 418). The people involved in revolutions may get caught up in the events of the moment and make bad decisions or oppress the people who were supposed to be liberated. Burke (1986) believed that slow and deliberate contemplation and ratification of a government by "great lawyers and great statesmen" was the best way to form a government (p. 100). He took great care not to endorse any particular form of government as long as it was derived through a slow and deliberate process with some input from the followers. It helped, Burke (1986) mentioned, that "those who will lead, must also, in a considerable degree, follow" (p. 128). He felt that these lessons were not being applied in France and the result would be serious negative consequences.

Other notable events of this period had an impact on the economy. The Copyright Act was passed in 1790 to protect the intellectual property of individuals. Assumption of war debt led states like Massachusetts to lower or repeal certain taxes on residents. A section of a paved road, the Philadelphia-Lancaster Turnpike, was opened and served as a model for development of other paved toll roads. Samuel Slater opened his first cotton mill in Rhode Island that utilized a machine and technology that Britain did not want anyone to have. It was built from memory and was a significant increase in productive output that would spur creation of huge textile industry in New England. Schlesinger (1993) added that this was "the beginning of the Industrial Revolution in America" (p. 158).

*Set 14 Perceived Task Complexity.* This set was the first two years of the new government under the Constitution. Economic and political reforms were such that Americans could begin to view the future more favorably. Agriculture was doing well, imports and exports were up, financial market reform meant that investors could expect to get a fair return, and the Industrial Revolution was just beginning. The score for this set was 3.17.

*Set 14 Structural Leadership Profile.* George Washington was elected the first President of the new government. His approach was a continuation of his leadership as a general but adjusted based on his experiences during and after the war. The score for this set was 3.00.

*Set 14 Structural Followership Profile.* The followers for this period were people like Madison and Jefferson who looked out for the interests of the public. Other followers were industrialists, farmers, and merchants who were looking to improve their lives now that the new government was in place. The score for this period was 3.19. The degree of congruence was 0.13.

*Set 14 Social Satisfaction Instrument.* There was an improved outlook for the first time in quite a while. There were no significant riots or rebellions and the economy improved. A new legislature and President were elected that represented the views of the followers. A new Congress was seated and therefore no turnover was used for this set. The score for this period was only from Section I and was 1.20.

*Set 15: 1791-1792.*

The events of this set consisted of actions that continued to build a new government and economy. It was also a time when differences between two influential officeholders began to polarize into two more distinct ideologies. The differences between Jefferson and Hamilton were aired in front of the masses as each took to the print media to battle each other. The citizens appeared to be very satisfied that the economy began on a path to solid growth.

Washington requested that Jefferson and Hamilton submit their arguments for and against the establishment of a Bank of the United States. The stage was set for confrontation as Hamilton argued for a loose interpretation of the Constitution while Jefferson petitioned for a narrow one. Cunningham (1987) added that "Jefferson's arguments for strict construction laid the foundation for the state's rights interpretation of the Constitution, while Hamilton's opinion served as the model that Chief Justice John Marshall would later follow in giving judicial sanction to the doctrine of implied powers" (pp. 164-165). Jefferson's argument was that anything not expressly dictated by the Constitution was prohibited by the federal government and thus was in the realm of the states or individuals. A national bank was not authorized and so any departure from the strict interpretation approach would open the door to much larger abuses of power by the federal government. Hamilton stated that what was and was not constitutional was "the *end* to which the measure [related] as a *mean*" (Cunningham, 1987, p. 167). Both the House and Senate approved the bill authorizing the bank. Washington accepted Hamilton's view and signed the bill into law on February 25, 1791.

The differences between Jefferson and Hamilton intensified when Jefferson and Madison began to circulate around New England to increase support for their Anti-Federalist, later to be known as Republican, views. Schlesinger (1993) asserted that this developing rift pitted Jefferson's "democratic agrarian society based on the individual freeholder and opposed to a strong centralized government" against Hamilton's "diversified industrial society governed by a strong central government of the elite" (p. 159).

The conflict moved into the newspapers as the pro-Jefferson *National Gazette* battled the pro-Hamilton *Gazette of the United States* for public opinion. Hamilton was particularly upset that Madison was against him because he and Madison had worked together to compose the majority of the Federalist Papers. The fighting grew so intense that Washington felt obliged to step in to the middle of them. Washington (1997) wrote to Hamilton that "differences in political opinions are as unavoidable as, to a certain point, they may perhaps be necessary" but that he and Jefferson should temper their arguments as it was regrettable that "Men of abilities – zealous patriots – having the same *general* objects in view" could not respect each other's beliefs (p. 819). He then turned to Jefferson and stated that "when some of the best Citizens in the United States – Men of discernment – Uniform and tried Patriots" have opposing views it would be ideal if they could do so with respect for the other's views (p. 826). John Adams strived to stay out of the fight. McCullough (2001) felt that Adams stayed loyal to Washington but was "nominally a Federalist, refusing to steadfastly be, or to be perceived as, a party man" (p. 434). The attacks between Jefferson and Madison on one side and Hamilton on the other continued through the end of the period.

Hamilton delivered the *Report on Manufactures* to Congress on December 5, 1791. Hamilton argued for the stimulation of domestic industry through tariffs, few restrictions on individuals so they can be productive, and protection of agriculture since they are vital export items. Mitchell (1999) stated that "in this report he gave his most explicit statement of his idea of what constituted national wealth" (p. 217). The end result Hamilton had in mind was a combination of agriculture with a robust manufacturing sector that could thrive in an economy of stable prices and solid credit.

Bryant and Dethloff (1990) added that Hamilton believed "the opportunities afforded by manufacturing … would promote immigration … and a spirit of enterprise and new opportunity" (p. 58).

The economy was on the mend in this set. Turnpike and canal construction began to increase as merchants and farmers pressed both government and private investors to build them in order to better facilitate commerce. The New York Stock Exchange was established in 1792 to provide a trading forum for select securities. The Coinage Act, passed by Congress, utilized gold and silver standard to back currency. Efforts to negotiate favorable trade relationships continued in Europe. The general population was content as Washington (1997) wrote to Gouverneur Morris that "the Farmer, the Merchant, and the Mechanic have seen their several interests attend to, and from thence they unite in placing a confidence in their representatives" and that "industry has there taken [the] place of idleness" (p. 784).

Not all citizens were content as opposition to the Whiskey Act, passed March 3, 1791 to raise revenue from liquor, increased notably in the southern states and in western Pennsylvania. The farmers were upset because the tax affected a lucrative practice in which they disposed of excess grain by converting it to alcohol. Washington felt compelled in late summer to warn farmers to pay the tax as he was committed to enforcement of it.

Thomas Paine published his response to Edmund Burke's *Reflections on the Revolution in France* in 1791. His main argument was against hereditary government because it imposed a tyrannical government on posterity. Paine (1984) stated that "the circumstances of the world are continually changing, and the opinions of men change also" so a government that is based on one period in time may not be applicable for another period (p. 45). This was essentially a contingency view of government based on the surrounding environment. Paine (1984) also put forth arguments that would be echoed later by Max Weber that "the exercise of Government requires talents and abilities" and citizens were bound only by laws and not men (pp. 140-143). The book was widely read among citizens as well as Jefferson and Adams. The views of Paine appeared to be consistent with mainstream American views.

Other notable events of this set included the addition of Vermont and Kentucky as states and the ratification of 10 of the 12 amendments to the Constitution. Washington was reelected for his second term as President at the end of 1792 while John Adams was reelected as Vice President.

*Set 15 Perceived Task Complexity.* The economy continued to improve as Congress, Washington, and his staff took steps to solidify the new government and stabilize the economy. Confidence grew from the prior set which tended to draw more resources, labor and capital, into the system for development and improvement of industry and agriculture. The score for this set was 3.25.

*Set 15 Structural Leadership Profile.* George Washington was reelected as President. His popularity was still very high among Americans as a result of his military past and his actions during the first term of his presidency. The score for this set was 3.00.

*Set 15 Structural Followership Profile.* Farmers, merchants, and industrial workers were the followers for this set. Many of the followers' views were expressed by

people like Thomas Jefferson, James Madison, Alexander Hamilton, and Thomas Paine.
The score for this set was 3.19. The degree of congruence was 0.17.

*Set 15 Social Satisfaction Instrument.* It appeared that Americans were satisfied
during this set. President Washington was reelected, Congressional turnover was
41.18%, Senate turnover was 50% among eligible seats, and increased confidence was a
general indication of an optimistic view of the future. The score for this set was 1.39.

*Set 16: 1793-1794.*

The conflict between Jefferson and Hamilton continued during this set further
defining the opposing political views of each. War in Europe created some uncertainties
for a new nation that struggled to stay out of the way. This external force combined with
some internal dissatisfaction was a test of the young nation's ability to survive.

The set began with an attack on Alexander Hamilton in his role as Secretary of
the Treasury. William Branch Giles, a Republican Virginia congressman, attempted to
continue the assault on the Federalists by questioning his integrity and so chose Hamilton
as his primary target. Charges were brought against Hamilton in both the House and
Senate that he acted outside the rules for his position when he authorized foreign loans.
The Senate was satisfied with Hamilton's responses to the questions put to him but the
House continued to press him further. Giles introduced measures that required intense
accounting in the hopes that the information would not be produced. Hamilton did so and
thus held them at bay through his thoroughness and the inability of many congressmen to
understand economics. Mitchell (1999) suggested that members of Congress "felt it was
demeaning to rely on" Hamilton to develop fiscal policy as he should be "no more than a
superior clerk and record keeper" (p. 261). Part of the reason for the rift was that it was a

continuation of the struggle for influence as to how the new nation should be shaped while others were dissatisfied due to an economic downturn related to real estate and stock speculation. Jefferson felt that the Republicans failed because there were more allies of Hamilton in Congress (Mitchell, 1999, p. 263).

War broke out between France and Britain in early 1793. The Federalists under Washington, Hamilton, and Adams sided with Britain while the Republicans under Jefferson and Madison favored the French. Washington proclaimed neutrality in April while Madison wondered whether the President had the "authority to issue such a proclamation without congressional approval" (Schlesinger, 1993, p. 163). Efforts to stay out of the war consumed a considerable amount of the administration's time as both France and Britain played the various factions in America off of each other in an attempt to gain whatever advantage they could. Jefferson did not advocate joining the conflict on the side of France but he did not like the idea of retarding the progress that was being made in France as a result of the revolution. Jefferson, in trying to influence Washington and Congress, "avoided open dispute, debate, controversy, or any kind of confrontation, but behind the scenes he was unrelenting and extremely effective" to the point that Adams thought of him as a "fanatic" (McCullough, 2001, pp. 442-443). Congress passed the Neutrality Act in June of 1794 to prevent Americans from joining the armies of France and Britain.

Jefferson decided that he no longer wanted to be Secretary of State. Jefferson wanted to resign at the end of Washington's first term but did not want to be seen as surrendering to Hamilton. Cunningham (1987) said that Jefferson could not help wondering "whether he had made the right decision, for his final year ... turned out to be one of the most arduous of his many years in public life" (p. 178). The decision was made by Jefferson to resign and he made it official on July 31, 1793 by submitting his resignation to Washington. His last day was December 31, 1793 and he was replaced by former Attorney General Edmund Randolph.

Jefferson, and many like him, was concerned about government's influence on the average citizen. His views were shared and clarified by writers of the time, especially Charles Brockden Brown. Brown wrote *Wieland*, a widely read novel, in which a person falls under the influence of voices and ends in the tragic deaths of people. The book hinted at how the virtue of individuals could be exploited in order to influence them and get them to do things they might possibly have not done on their own. The very first line of the story begins "I feel little reluctance in complying with your request" (Brown, 1991, p. 5). Many like Jefferson and Madison felt that giving too much power to individuals without adequate checks and balances was hazardous as they could fall under the control of an influential yet dangerous person. This view remained a basis of the Republican's strict interpretation view of the Constitution.

There were other notable events of this set aside from the conflict between Federalists and Republicans. Congress passed the Fugitive Slave Act in 1793 that facilitated the return of runaway slaves to their owners. They then turned around and passed a law in 1794 that prevented slave trade with foreign nations. The slave issue would continue to be a hot issue between slave owners and abolitionists.

Violence broke out in western Pennsylvania as farmers burned the homes of tax collectors and tarred and feathered revenue officers (Schlesinger, 1993, p. 165). Washington (1997) responded with a proclamation calling for the militia to intervene because "combinations to defeat the execution of the laws laying duties upon spirits distilled within the United States" were unlawful and should be suppressed (pp. 870-872). It was over by September as the use of force was enough to send many home. Some of the rebels were arrested, a handful were tried, and only a few were convicted. The convicted were eventually pardoned.

Improvements to economic resources took the form of education and organization for labor, as well as structural aspects. Samuel Slater developed Sunday School to teach reading, writing, and math to children who worked in his textile factories. Shoemakers organized into the first American trade union in Philadelphia. The Middlesex Canal in New England, another major canal was under construction in South Hadley Falls, Massachusetts, and the Philadelphia-Lancaster turnpike completion spurred the development and building of more paved toll roads. John Jay negotiated what was known as the Jay Treaty with Britain, which provided for improved commercial ties, the withdrawal of British troops from occupied American territory, and settlement of debts owed to loyalists and other British citizens.

*Set 16 Perceived Task Complexity.* Real estate and stock speculation combined with trade disruption due to the war between England and France. These were not enough to prevent progress toward economic improvements in education, labor organization, and transportation. Relations improved with Britain toward the end of the set. The score for this period was 3.17.

*Set 16 Structural Leadership Profile.* George Washington was consistent in his role as President and the actions that he took. He remained focused on the precedent that he set as the first of what he hoped would be a long line of Presidents. The score for this set remained 3.00.

*Set 16 Structural Followership Profile.* Thomas Jefferson, James Madison, Alexander Hamilton, merchants, and industrialists provided input for this set's profile. The public appeared to be divided between strict and loose interpretations of the Constitution. The dispute that existed though was not serious enough to warrant a change in the form of the government but was simply one of healthy debate. The score for this set remained the same at 3.19.

*Set 16 Social Satisfaction Instrument.* Americans appeared to be reasonably content in this set. There continued to be a search for the ideal interpretation of the Constitution but there was only one major conflict over taxes. Congressional turnover was 58.56% and Senate turnover was 45.45% among eligible seats. The score for this set was 1.59.

*Summary of Results.*

The results from all 16 sets were summarized in this section. The scatterplot, linear regression, and Pearson Correlation were calculated and included as well. The discussion of results follows in Chapter V.

A summary of set instruments can be found in Table 7. The Set #, PTC, Structural Leadership Profile (SLP), Structural Followership Profile (SFP), Congruency, and Social Satisfaction are listed. The Largest Difference and Smallest Difference are the difference between the largest and smallest of the PTC, SLP, and SFP scores for each set. They were added as an additional means of analysis. The range, minimum, maximum, mean, and standard deviation were also added to enhance analysis.

<h3 align="center">Table 7 - Summary of Set Instruments</h3>

| Set # | PTC | SLP | SFP | Largest difference | Smallest difference | Congruency | Social Satisfaction |
|---|---|---|---|---|---|---|---|
| 1 | 2.83 | 1.80 | 3.44 | 1.64 | 1.03 | 1.09 | 2.60 |
| 2 | 2.67 | 1.80 | 3.81 | 2.01 | 0.87 | 1.34 | 3.20 |
| 3 | 2.83 | 1.80 | 3.81 | 2.01 | 1.03 | 1.34 | 3.40 |
| 4 | 2.92 | 1.80 | 3.75 | 1.95 | 1.12 | 1.30 | 2.80 |
| 5 | 2.83 | 1.75 | 3.75 | 2.00 | 1.08 | 1.33 | 2.80 |
| 6 | 2.50 | 1.65 | 3.94 | 2.29 | 0.85 | 1.53 | 3.20 |
| 7 | 3.08 | 2.78 | 3.62 | 0.84 | 0.30 | 0.56 | 1.88 |
| 8 | 3.08 | 3.63 | 3.31 | 0.55 | 0.23 | 0.36 | 2.25 |
| 9 | 3.00 | 3.53 | 3.19 | 0.53 | 0.19 | 0.35 | 2.25 |
| 10 | 3.08 | 3.40 | 3.19 | 0.32 | 0.11 | 0.10 | 2.14 |
| 11 | 3.17 | 3.65 | 3.13 | 0.52 | 0.04 | 0.35 | 2.85 |
| 12 | 2.83 | 3.52 | 3.13 | 0.69 | 0.30 | 0.46 | 3.11 |
| 13 | 3.00 | 3.55 | 3.13 | 0.55 | 0.13 | 0.37 | 2.67 |
| 14 | 3.17 | 3.00 | 3.19 | 0.19 | 0.02 | 0.13 | 1.20 |
| 15 | 3.25 | 3.00 | 3.19 | 0.25 | 0.06 | 0.17 | 1.39 |
| 16 | 3.17 | 3.00 | 3.19 | 0.19 | 0.02 | 0.13 | 1.59 |

<h3 align="center">Statistical summary</h3>

| | PTC | SLP | SFP | Largest difference | Smallest difference | Congruency | Social Satisfaction |
|---|---|---|---|---|---|---|---|
| Max: | 3.25 | 3.65 | 3.94 | 2.29 | 1.12 | 1.53 | 3.40 |
| Min: | 2.50 | 1.65 | 3.13 | 0.19 | 0.02 | 0.10 | 1.20 |
| Range: | 0.75 | 2.00 | 0.81 | 2.10 | 1.10 | 1.43 | 2.20 |
| Mean: | 2.96 | 2.73 | 3.42 | 1.03 | 0.46 | 0.68 | 2.46 |
| Std. dev: | 0.20 | 0.81 | 0.30 | 0.79 | 0.44 | 0.53 | 0.68 |

The min and max values for the PTC were 3.25 and 2.50, with a range of 0.75. One standard deviation from either side of the mean of 3.00 was 0.50, which meant that the environment, although shifting from one side of the mean to the other, never changed from average complexity. The standard deviation of all PTC scores was 2.00, which indicated that the environment was fairly stable.

The min and max values for the SLP were 3.65 and 1.65, with a range of 2.00. The low value of 1.65 was the extremely autocratic leadership of King George III and the 3.65 was the democratic leadership that occurred right after the end of the Revolutionary War. The range of 2.00 reflects the change from autocracy in the beginning to a moderately democratic leadership. The mean of 2.73 was fairly close to where leadership finally ended in 1794. The range of +/- one standard deviation from the mean was from 2.50 to 3.50 so it would be reasonable to state that leadership, especially in the last 8 years was moderately democratic.

The min and max values for SFP were 3.94 and 3.13, with a range of 0.81. The followership never moved to the left of the central mean of 3.00 but did shift a few times beyond one standard deviation (3.50) into the democratic area for a brief period before shifting back toward the mean and settling in the moderately democratic area just right of central or mixed leadership. The standard deviation of all followership scores was 0.30, which indicated that the followers' styles were for the most part within one standard deviation. This would indicate that their styles were fairly stable over the 32 year period.

The largest and smallest differences among all three scores were included in Table 7. Figure 6 shows a graphical depiction of the differences plotted over the 16 sets. It is not the calculation of congruence; rather it is simply a brief overview that displays a similar relationship. The differences between any had the largest gap in the early part of the study and represented a big difference between one or more score within each set. The gap narrowed and declined toward the end of the study. The major decline in differences began with the year that independence was declared and progressively declined to a very narrow gap.

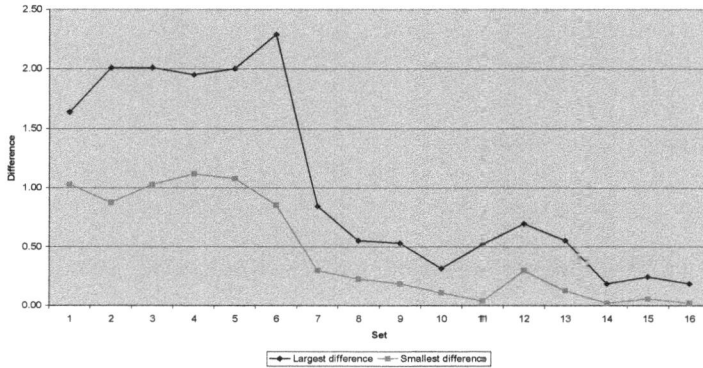

Figure 6 - Comparison of Differences

Figure 7 shows the scatterplot of congruence and social satisfaction complete with

a regression curve.

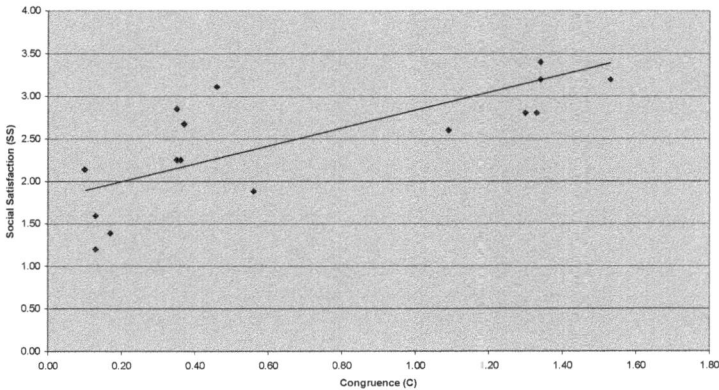

Figure 7 - Social Satisfaction / Congruence Scatterplot

The linear regression calculation of the relationship between congruence and

social satisfaction is 0.7335. It is reflected in the upward sloping direction of the

regression curve in Figure 7. The relationship thus established can be illustrated as:

SS = a + b ( C ), where (3)

SS = Social Satisfaction

a = y-intercept, or 1,81638

b = slope of regression line, or 0.941145

C = Congruence of the task environment, leadership style, and followership style.

The user of the three instruments would simply take the congruence of the scores as calculated in Table 1 and insert it into formula 3 using the established values to calculate the degree of Social Satisfaction one could expect with the results of administered instruments.

The Pearson Correlation among congruence and social satisfaction was calculated using formula 2 in Chapter III and was determined to be 0.538. The Pearson Correlation is a measure of strength among relationships and varies from 0.00, or no relationship, to 1.00 or a complete and direct relationship. The Pearson for this study, while not very strong was not weak either. It was determined that the relationship was moderately strong. Social satisfaction is dependent to a moderate extent based on the congruence between the styles and the environment. The results would indicate that something else may be working with the congruence to determine satisfaction. More discussion follows in Chapter V.

Chapter V – Appetite satisfied?

Discussion of the results began with an emphasis on how well they fit with the assertions of each researcher. Other conclusions were drawn as well and were included as part of an overall analysis. Recommendations for today's leaders should allow them to understand their followers and environment in such a way as to ensure a higher probability of satisfaction. Areas for further research were provided as a means to enhance the conclusions.

*Discussion.*

A brief review of each researcher's assertions combined with the results in Chapter IV confirmed or refuted their conclusions. The common theme among the researchers, as stated in Chapter II, was the existence of a continuum for leadership and followership styles and the task environment ranging from simple, authoritarian, or autocratic to complex, participative, or democratic.

Max Weber's theory touched on aspects for leaders, followers, and the organizational structure. Rules and procedures should be based on consensus, expediency, and relevancy to the tasks to be completed. The colonists were unable to have input into the taxes levied on them and could not see the relevancy of their purpose. When independence was achieved they were able to have input through an elected Congress and their right to express their views through voting and demonstrations were able to ensure that any levies were relevant. This was a grievance system that Weber said was needed in order for the organization to operate effectively.

Weber's theory also suggested that rules and laws should be abstract enough to allow flexibility and should not be shaped to a particular person. The rigid laws of Parliament and King George III were replaced by the Articles of Confederation and the Constitution. The Articles were so vague and flexible that very few things were accomplished. The Constitution was somewhat less vague yet still flexible via Supreme Court interpretation. Americans no longer had to adhere to one man's rule but instead followed the Constitution. This provided for equality among all Americans since there was little possibility of favoritism.

Another of Weber's conclusions was that the leaders should be selected for their positions based on their qualifications to fill the office. Although it remained possible that inexperienced or unqualified persons could be elected as President or members of Congress the probability of that was low. Americans believed that King George III was not the ideal leader they needed but were unable to replace him through the existing system. That changed with their independence.

Mary Parker Follett's theory suggested that leaders should have knowledge of the tasks involved, the ability to see the whole picture and understand the relevancy between the various factors as they were affected by dynamic external forces. The Americans felt that King George III and Parliament did not understand their environment and would not allow adequate representation to ensure that they did. The new government under the Constitution was able to do so and adapt to changing external forces like the war in Europe and the subsequent interruption of trade. Congress was not hindered in its efforts to deal with changes by the states, as happened with the government under the Articles of

Confederation.    The Americans under the Constitution became responsible followers by exercising their right to vote.

Taylor's Scientific Management added structural insight to this work that applied to all types of organizations no matter where they were on the autocratic-democratic continuum.  The structure of tasks should be based on relevant information required to do the tasks and nothing more.  The Constitution was set up to accomplish only the necessary tasks of protection of life and property, justice, and the promotion of happiness.

Taylor suggested that followers should be selected based on how well they fit with the organization requirements.  This was not possible with a country without resorting to unethical means.  Taylor also indicated that leaders and followers should be given responsibility to accomplish the goals and objectives and the followers should hold the leaders accountable for their part.  All these requirements were not present prior to ratification of the Constitution.  The level of satisfaction on the part of leaders and followers increased productivity and appeared to be the case toward the end of the study.

Douglas McGregor's Theory X and Theory Y emphasized that leaders should organize resources in such a way that allows followers to satisfy their own needs.  This was not possible under the colonial system and the Americans were very dissatisfied. The new government under the Articles and Constitution provided the resources for them to do so.  One problem with this theory was the difficulty in satisfying all needs of the followers due to the scarcity of resources and logistics concerns.  The Constitution provided a means to satisfy most needs through compromise.  This was far better than the Articles of Confederation that tried to appease all but was unable to accomplish much.

Jay Lorsch suggested that there was no one best organizational structure. The colonial government worked for a while up to the mid-eighteenth century. Dynamic external forces such as a growing American population that slowly gained the ability to produce for itself the things it needed increased pressure for a new system.

Lorsch required the incorporation of a conflict resolution process in the organization structure in order to deal with any problems that may arise regarding interaction between leaders, followers, and the organization. The conflict resolution process did not exist in the colonial government but made its way into the Constitution.

Chris Argyris indicated that an individual's personality development began at a passive and dependent state and progressed toward an active and independent state. The colonists began as dependents of Britain and required its assistance for most of their needs. They had no real problems with this system. This dependence began to change over time as economic development lessened the need for reliance on Britain. Americans learned to be more independent and expressed increasing amounts of dissatisfaction as the colonial system rubbed up against their changing needs. Progress along the dependent-independent continuum occurred over time usually in small increments. Attempts by the King and Parliament to pull the colonists back toward dependency met with increasing levels of frustration.

The task environment remained in the mixed area and thus determined that the followers needed a mixed type of government, which they eventually developed. Congruency between the Americans' styles and the organization's mixed task environment eventually led to decent performance toward the end of the set. The theory stated that organizations need to be designed or redesigned with the Americans' styles in mind, which was done in the form of the Constitution.

Rensis Likert said that a person's growth needs were derived from their personality while achievement of their needs determined satisfaction. The achievement of their goals outlined in the Constitution decreased the level of dissatisfaction that existed from the colonial and Articles of Confederation governments. Likert also felt that required changes to the organizational design due to external forces needed to consider how the growth needs of leaders and followers will be affected. A Constitutional Convention composed of followers was able to match the needs of Americans with the necessary functions that only a unified government could provide.

David Frew's theory stated that each person has both a leadership and followership style that fall on a continuum ranging from autocratic to democratic types. He also felt that people are influenced by their personalities that are relatively stable over time. The leadership of Americans ranged from the autocratic King George III to the democratic government under the Articles of Confederation. The followers were mostly a mixed type that was slightly to the right of the mean in the moderately democratic style. The Constitution brought the government back toward the followers' style. The success of America hinged on the satisfaction that leaders and followers perceived as a result of the degree of fit between each other and the task environment.

Personalities are relatively stable over time and it was futile to try to change a person's personality to fit the task environment as was evidenced by the fact that follower styles did not change much but a government composed of leaders was brought into being that were congruent. This required a change in leadership.

Tannenbaum and Schmidt also agreed that personality influenced behavior and was relatively stable. Their leader determined how much freedom to give the followers as King George III did. Tannenbaum and Schmidt said a leader did this based on the followers' experience, the leader's perception of the follower's need for independence and their ability to handle responsibility, as well as how much power a leader wanted to retain. King George III felt that he knew best but it turned out that he did not. It was ultimately the followers who knew best as they designed their own ideal government and got a workable one on the second try that increased satisfaction.

Another aspect of the research from Tannenbaum and Schmidt was that sudden changes or big movements in a leader's style may upset followers as they are used to a given leader style. King George III's style moved toward the autocratic end as his patience with the Americans got low. He was trying to pull them back toward autocracy. This increased the level of dissatisfaction of Americans and led to their declaration of independence.

Thomas Hobbes asserted that any particular form of government was just as long as it was voluntarily entered into to by the followers and was implemented by the designated leaders as intended. The colonists did not feel King George III was just in his actions and thus sought change. They brought about a government of their own design that allowed them to change leaders if they did not follow the rules set forth in the Constitution.

John Locke's theory of government suggested that there were two ends of a continuum with respect to the amount of governance that an individual encountered. The despotic end was characterized by the absence of rights, property, and many rules that were enacted and executed at the sole discretion of the leader. King George III did not respect the rights and property of colonists as he levied taxes without consent, stationed troops in their homes, and closed ports to shipping at will. The State of Nature end of the continuum was characterized by the absence of any rules, all rights were reserved by each individual, and property was owned and protected by each person. The government under the Articles of Confederation approached this end and the result was a lack of coordination and not much success in getting anything done.

Locke stated that rights and property were voluntarily given up by individuals in a contractual agreement to a leader or governing body in exchange for protection of their property and or for a reduction in anxiety they may have over uncertainty that exists in the environment. The Americans agreed to give up some of the freedom gained under the Articles of Confederation in order to get things accomplished. They realized that too much freedom was a hindrance. It also bordered on anarchy. Followers would not normally move backward on the continuum away from the State of Nature unless they received some greater benefit. Efforts to move them backward would be met with resistance.

Analysis of all sets revealed that when the leadership and followership styles were closely aligned with each other and the task environment satisfaction would be high. This was an important finding because it did not matter what type of government was in place as long as there was congruence. The high degree of congruence during sets eight through eleven had low satisfaction due to the fact that Americans viewed the structure as ideal but did not initially see that it was too democratic and was getting in the way.

The results appear to diminish the contingency view of leadership where leaders are able to adjust their styles by moving back and forth along the continuum to align with current needs. It seems that personality and styles are relatively stable. The followers' styles did not vary much over 32 years, confirmation of the views held by Argyris (1987), Frew (1977, 1981) and Likert (1987). The leaders would not be able to move more than one standard deviation over a short period of time and it would not be possible for one to move much more than one standard deviation over the long run, even if influenced by dramatic events. Just as important is the fact that movements along the continuum over time are generally rightward from autocracy to democracy. One may expect that leftward movements beyond one standard deviation will be met with resistance and frustration.

The Americans were not satisfied with the leadership of King George III and he was unwilling or unable to change to adapt to their needs. The Congress under the Articles of Confederation was too democratic and was close to anarchy. The followers chose a government more closely aligned to their needs and the result was satisfaction. They gave up some of their rights only because they received a benefit equal to what they gave up. The benefit was a functional government that intruded in each person's life only enough to accomplish its objectives and no more.

Since the task environment and the followers' styles were difficult to change over a period of time the only thing that could be done to bring about satisfaction was to change the leader. Selection of the leader should be done in such a way that will result in the closest fit. This led to an unexpected additional conclusion. The leader acts as a fulcrum, if you will, that acts to balance the needs of the followers and the goals and objectives of the organization. The followers and organization are acted upon by external forces in the environment. The external forces act differently on each of the needs, goals,

and objectives and thus require only one type of leadership that varies only within one

standard deviation.

## Figure 8 - Fulcrum of leadership

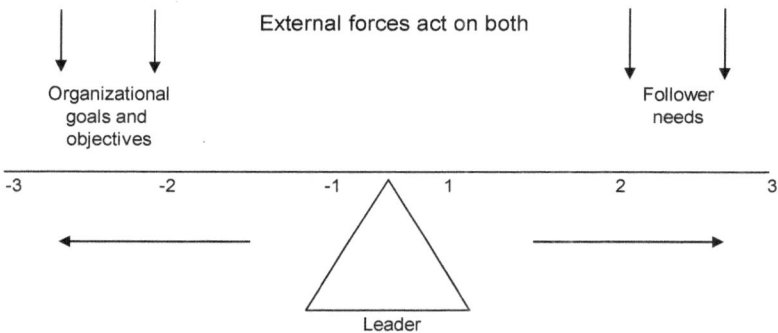

Figure 8 shows a graphical display of what I shall refer to as the Fulcrum of

Leadership. The leader is the fulcrum and is capable of moving one standard deviation in

either direction because of the stability of his or her personality. The fulcrum is a good

example because it can only move a little in either direction as well before an imbalance

results. A dramatic change in either or both the organization and followers usually is

brought about by external forces and would require a new leader or government if the

change requires a large movement to restore stability.

A second unexpected conclusion was that movements, if any, along the

continuum should generally be unidirectional. Figure 9 depicts a satisfaction curve that I

expect one may realize with movements of followers along the continuum. Followers

generally move to the right over time from autocracy to democracy as it is more difficult to remove independence from a follower or leader as it is to add independence. Increased levels of satisfaction should be the result. However, as the democratic end is approached the level of satisfaction begins to decline again as anarchy is approached. This occurs because protection of one's self and property falls to each individual. Some may be unable to do so and would be subject to the tyranny of the strongest. Such a system will naturally increase dissatisfaction.

**Figure 9 - Satisfaction curve**

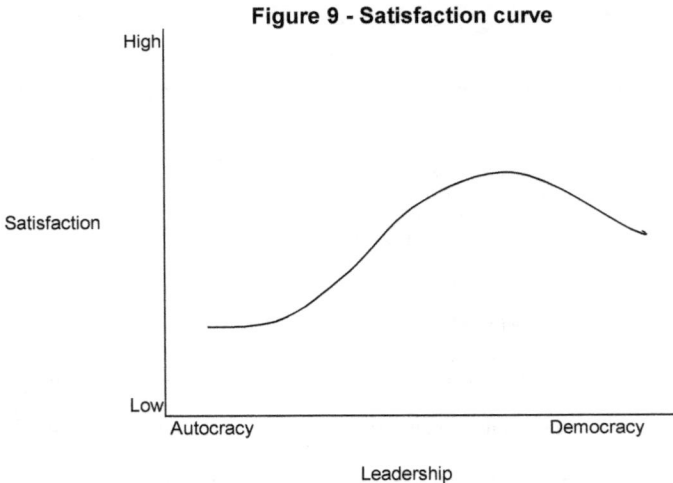

One additional comment should be noted on the satisfaction curve. It is not necessary that movement occur. Followers may stay in one place indefinitely if the external forces allow them to. Movement is not a requirement.

*Summary of conclusions.*

Leadership and followership styles are based on personality. Personality is relatively stable over time and generally only varies by one standard deviation in either direction. It generally only develops in one direction toward democracy.

The task environment exerts influence over an organization and its leaders and followers. An organization may change its goals and objectives based on the influences in the environment. The followers will also change their needs based on the influences in the environment, but are limited by their personality as to how much the needs will change over a short period of time. The leader's style is influenced by personality and is relatively stable over time in the same manner as the followers. This limits the leader's ability to move back and forth by changing styles. The result is that if a change in leadership style is required due to changes in the organization or follower it may be necessary to change the leader rather than expect that he or she can move to an area where the degree of fit is fairly close. The fit is the congruence of the leader, follower, and organization. Ultimately, then, leaders are expendable and more likely the most irrelevant aspect of the four factors of satisfaction: leadership, followership, the environment, and the structure.

It also appears that a certain amount of dissatisfaction is present at all times as the social satisfaction never fell below 1.00. This makes sense as a complete lack of dissatisfaction would imply a group of individuals so happy that they would be euphoric. Such a state is generally only present in the imaginary world of Utopia. George Washington once stated that content followers do not force change unless personally affected by some aspect of the environment. A group of individuals will never be completely satisfied and as such complete satisfaction should never be a goal. A relative degree of satisfaction is the end result that organizational leadership professionals should strive to achieve.

The Fulcrum of Leadership and the Satisfaction Curve were not expected when this research was begun. They gradually evolved as the analysis drew to a conclusion but it appears to be a valid working model of how the three groups interact. A new definition of leadership is then possible. I argue that leadership can be described as:

The ability to balance the needs of the followers with the organizational goals and objectives as they are constantly influenced by dynamic external forces.

*Recommendations for today's leaders.*

Today's leaders, no matter what type of organization they part of, can gain some insight from this research. It is important to understand that personality determines both leadership and followership styles. This means that the styles are relatively stable over time. The leader's role then is to understand what type of styles the followers have, what the level of task complexity is, and whether there is congruence between all three. If the leader is causing dissatisfaction because he or she does not fit the organization he or she may need to be replaced with one who does fit well.

Selection of followers is not possible in the case of a country but in a workplace environment the followers can be selected in such a way that they will fit well with the task environment. The leader's remaining role is to move back and forth within one standard deviation to keep the needs of the followers in balance with the organization's goals and objectives.

The wars in Afghanistan and Iraq present a unique situation for new governments. Americans are generally in favor of democracy no matter what the case. This approach may increase problems instead of solving them. Simple task environments like Afghanistan and moderately simple task environments that may be found in Iraq should be matched with follower and leader styles. The followers appear to expect a certain level of autocracy and may not know how to act in a democracy. They probably fit well with a simple or moderately simple task environment. Any attempt to establish a government and select a leader that are too democratic may only increase frustration and undo any good intentions the Americans may have. Careful analysis of the conclusions in this paper should help in the design and implementation of a new government.

*Possible ways to build a better salad.*

There are two areas that may be further explored to enhance the conclusions in this research. Refinement of the instruments and additional research into what factors influence satisfaction should increase the likelihood that those who attempt to influence satisfaction may be able to do so.

The analysis of the sets utilized the instruments in the appendix to describe or interpret what was going on. They should not be relied on solely to analyze a situation. Qualitative analysis is as important or more important. The instruments should be viewed as a second set of tools. The instruments used in this research may need to be modified in order to apply them to countries or other unique situations. That was a limitation of this research even though the results turned out well. Design of the Social Satisfaction Instrument should focus more on those things that affect satisfaction.

Additional research in the areas of what leads to satisfaction can add to the degree of fit in order to come up with a multiple regression analysis that could bring forth a higher Pearson Correlation than 0.53. Simple regression using only the congruence was a

good start but certainly there are other factors that influence satisfaction. The researcher

that discovers those aspects and adds them to congruence should be able to utilize

multiple regression as an additional tool.

References

Adams, S. (1769, February 27). Right of Revolution. *Boston Gazette.* Retrieved

September 14, 2002 from http://press-pubs.uch:cago.edu/founders/documents

v1ch3s4.html.

Arbnor, I. & Bjerke, B. (1997). *Methodology for creating business knowledge*

(2nd ed.). Thousand Oaks, CA: Sage Publications.

Argyris, C. (1987). The individual and organization: Some problems of mutual

adjustment. In L. Boone & D. Bowen (Ed.), *The great writings in management*

*and organizational behavior.* 2$^{nd}$ ed. (pp. 139-158). New York: McGraw-Hill.

Bailyn, B. (1992). The ideological origins of the American revolution.

Cambridge, MA: Harvard University Press.

British Parliament. (1764). The Currency Act of 1764. Retrieved September 14, 2002

from http://ahp.gatech.edu/currency_act_1764.html.

British Parliament. (1764). The Sugar Act. Retrieved September 16, 2002 from

http://ahp.gatech.edu/sugar_act_bp_1764.html.

Brown, C. B.. (1991). Wieland and Memoirs of Carwin the Biloquist.

New York: Penguin Books.

Burke, E. (1986). Reflections on the revolution in France. New York: Penguin

Books.

Bryant, K. L. & Dethloff, H. C. (1990). A history of American business

(2$^{nd}$ ed.). Englewood Cliffs, NJ: Prentice-Hall.

Copleston, F., S.J. (1959). A history of philosophy: Volume V – modern

philosophy. New York: Doubleday.

Cunningham, N. E. Jr. (1987). In pursuit of reason – The life of Thomas Jefferson. New York: Ballantine Books.

Descartes, R. (1996). *Discourse on method and related writings.* Desmond M. Clarke, Trans.). London: Penguin Classics. (Originally work published 1637).

Edwards, J. (1996). Sinners in the hands of an angry God. John Jeffery Fanella (Ed.). Phillipsburg, NJ: P&R Publishing Co.

Ellis, J. J. (2002). Founding brothers – the revolutionary generation. New York: Vintage Books.

Frew, D. R. (1977, February). Leadership and followership. *Personnel Journal*, 90-97.

Frew, D. R. (1981, November). Diagnosing and dealing with task complexity. *Personnel Administrator*, 87-92.

Follett, M. P. (1987). The essentials of leadership. In L. Boone & D. Bowen (Ed.), *The great writings in management and organizational behavior.* 2nd ed. (pp. 49-59). New York: McGraw-Hill.

Franklin, B. (1994). The autobiography of Benjamin Franklin. New York: Barnes & Noble Books.

Gerth, H. H. & Mills, C. W. (Eds.). (1973). *From Max Weber: Essays in sociology.* New York: Oxford University Press.

Giere, R. N. (1995). Science without laws of nature. In Friedel Weinert (Ed.). Laws of Nature: Essays on the philosophical, scientific, and historical dimensions. (pp. 120-138). Berlin: Walter de Gruyter, Inc.

Gephart, R. (n.d.). Paradigms and research methods. Retrieved 5 Jan 2004, from
 http://www.aom.pace.edu/rmd/1999_RMD_Forum_Paradigms_and_Research
 Methods.htm.

Hibbert, C. (1998). George III. New York: Basic Books.

House of Representatives of Massachusetts. (1765). Resolutions of the House of
 Rpresentatives of Massachusetts. Retrieved on September 14, 2002 from
 http://press-pubs.uchicago.edu/founders/print_documents/v1ch17s11.html.

House of Representatives of Massachusetts. (1768). Circular Letter to the Colonial
 Legislatures. Retrieved on September 14, 2002 from http://press-pubs.uchicago.
 edu/founders/print_documents/v1ch17s13.html.

Kant, I. (1990). Critique of pure reason. (J. M. D. Mecklejohn, Trans.).
 Amherst, NY: Prometheus Books.

Kesler, C. R. (Ed.). (1961). The Federalist Papers. New York: Penguin Putnam.

Ketcham, R. (Ed.). (1986). The Anti-Federalist Papers and the Constitutional
 Convention debates. New York: Mentor.

King George III. (1763). The royal proclamation. Retrieved September 14, 2002,
 from http://www.solon.org/Constitutions/Canada/English/PreConfederation/
 rp_1763.html.

Kuhn, T. S. (1996). The structure of scientific revolutions. (3rd ed.). Chicago:
 The University of Chicago Press.

Langguth, A. J. (1988). Patriots – the men who started the American Revolution.
 New York: Touchstone.

Lawler, E. E. III and Porter, L. W. (1987). The effect of performance on

job satisfaction. In L. Boone & D. Bowen (Ed.), *The great writings in*

*management and organizational behavior.* 2<sup>nd</sup> ed. (pp. 431-442). New York:

McGraw-Hill.

Lee, R. H. (1764). Richard Henry Lee to ------. Retrieved September 14,

2002 from http://press-pubs.uchicago.edu/founders/print_documents/v1ch17s10.

html.

Likert, R. (1987). An integrating principle and an overview. In L. Boone &

D. Bowen (Ed.), *The great writings in management and organizational*

*behavior.* 2<sup>nd</sup> ed. (pp.216-238). New York: McGraw-Hill.

Locke, J. (1988). Two treatises of government. (Peter Laslett, Ed.). Cambridge,

U.K.: Cambridge University Press.

Lorsch, J. W. (1987). Introduction to the structural design of organizations. In L.

Boone & D. Bowen (Ed.), *The great writings in management and organizational*

*behavior.* 2<sup>nd</sup> ed. (pp. 200-214). New York: McGraw-Hill.

McCullough, D. (2001). John Adams. New York: Simon & Schuster.

McGregor, D. M. (1987). The human side of enterprise. In L. Boone & D. Bowen

(Ed.), *The great writings in management and organizational behavior.* 2<sup>nd</sup> ed.

(pp. 126-136). New York: McGraw-Hill.

Mitchell, B. (1999). Alexander Hamilton – A concise biography. New York:

Barnes & Noble Books.

Newton, Sir I. (1962a). Principia: *Vol. I the system of the world.* (Andrew
Motte, Trans.). Berkeley, CA: University of California Press. (Original
work published 1729).

Newton, Sir I. (1962b). Principia: *Vol. II the system of the world.* (Andrew
Motte, Trans.). Berkeley, CA: University of California Press. (Original
work published 1729).

Otis, J. (1764). The rights of the British colonies asserted and proved. Retrieved
September 14, 2002 from http://press-pubs.uchicago.edu/founders/print_docu-
ments/v1ch2s5.html.

Paine, T. (1997). Common sense. Toronto: Dover Publications.

Paine, T. (1984). Rights of man. New York: Penguin Books.

Robson, C. (2002). Real world research. 2nd ed. Malden, MA: Blackwell
Publishing Ltd.

Raphael, R. (2002). A people's history of the American Revolution. New York:
HarperCollins.

Scandura, T. A. & Williams, E. A. (2000). Research methodology in management:
Current practices, trends, and implications for future research.
*Academy of Management Journal*, 43(6), 1248-1264.

Schein, E. (1990). Organizational culture. *American Psychologist.* 45(2), 109-119.

Schlesinger, A. M. (Ed.). (1993). The almanac of American history. Greenwich,
CT: Barnes & Noble Books.

Tannenbaum, R & Schmidt, W. H. (1987). How to choose a leadership

Pattern. In L. Boone & D. Bowen (Ed.), *The great writings in management*

*and organizational behavior.* 2$^{nd}$ ed. (pp. 262-278). New York: McGraw-Hill.

Taylor, F. W. (1987). The principles of scientific management. In L.

Boone & D. Bowen (Ed.), *The great writings in management and organizational*

*behavior.* 2$^{nd}$ ed. (pp. 32-47). New York: McGraw-Hill.

Washington, G. (1997). George Washington – writings. New York: Library of

America.

Weber, M. (1987). Legitimate authority and bureaucracy. In L. Boone & D. Bowen

(Ed.), *The great writings in management and organizational behavior.* 2$^{nd}$ ed.

(pp. 5-17). New York: McGraw-Hill.

Yukl, G. (2002). Leadership in organizations. Upper Saddle River, NJ:

Prentice Hall.

APPENDIX

Social Satisfaction Instrument

# SOCIAL SATISFACTION INSTRUMENT

Developed by Jim Triplett

## Section I

Answer the following questions, in general terms, by indicating how society would feel about each.

1) The outlook for the future is:

| hopeful | 0 | 1 | 2 | 3 | 4 discouraging |

2) Life is

| satisfying | 0 | 1 | 2 | 3 | 4 unsatisfying |

3) Government is mostly:

| responsive | 0 | 1 | 2 | 3 | 4 unresponsive |

4) Degree of control over one's life is:

| complete | 0 | 1 | 2 | 3 | 4 none |

5) The belief is that subsequent generations will be:

| better off | 0 | 1 | 2 | 3 | 4 worse off |

Score by averaging the five responses and enter here: _____

## Section II

1) House of Representatives turnover

For each election in a given time frame, calculate the following:
- a) # of newly elected congressional members
- b) # of seats up for election
- c) divide a by b
- d) multiply c by 4
- e) enter the average for the time frame _____

2) Senate turnover

For each election in a given time frame, calculate the following:
- a) # of newly elected Senate members
- b) # of seats up for election
- c) divide a by b
- d) multiply c by 4
- e) enter the average for the time frame _____

3) Because the House of Representatives can be turned over 100% while the Senate is limited to only 33%, calculate Section II value as follows:
- a) enter value from 1e _____
- b) multiply by 0.67 _____
- c) enter value from 2e _____
- d) multiply by 0.33 _____
- e) add b and d, enter here _____

## Section III

Multiply final value in Section I and Section II by 0.50 and add the results. This is the value of social satisfaction for the given time frame.

Section I value x 0.50 _____
Section II value x 0.50 _____
Total _____

## About the Author

James Triplett is a financial and risk management analyst at Dismal Realities, a Professor of Finance and Economics at Strayer University, an undergraduate and graduate management faculty member at University of Phoenix Cleveland, OH, Pittsburgh and Harrisburg, PA, Chattanooga & Nashville, TN, Online and Axia College of University of Phoenix, and an adjunct business instructor at Lakeland Community College in Kirtland, OH. He received his Bachelor of Arts in Management (Finance and Human Resource Management) from Mercyhurst College, a Master of Business Administration (Finance) from Gannon University, a Master of Science in Organizational Leadership from Mercyhurst College, and an ABD in Organization and Management at Capella University where he is working on completion of his doctoral dissertation, titled Organizational Design and Al-Qaeda ( A Case Study of the Structure of a Fundamentalist Islamic Terror Network), for his PhD in Organization and Management (Leadership) at Capella University. James is also author of Organizational Design: A holistic view ISBN: 978-0-615-14260-9.

www.ingramcontent.com/pod-product-compliance
Lightning Source LLC
Chambersburg PA
CBHW031930190326
41519CB00007B/480